The Living Kitchen

Sierra Club Books
TOOLS FOR TODAY

The economic climate is changing in this country, and a social transformation is occurring too. The resource shortage has caught up with us, and we must find new ways to enhance our lives. But how? Tools for Today are guides for this transitional period. They describe options and suggest strategies that can lead to more self-sufficient living. How to rethink, refurbish, and refit. How to gain access to new systems and human-scale technologies. How to have more in human terms as the times become economically harder. The projects in these books are for the individual, the family, and the community. They're money saving, they're practical, they're ecologically sound, and they look to a bright future.

Books in This Series

The Living Kitchen by Sharon Cadwallader
Your Affordable Solar Home by Dan Hibshman

Sierra Club Books
TOOLS FOR TODAY

The Living Kitchen

by Sharon Cadwallader

illustrated by Bill Prochnow

Sierra Club Books

San Francisco

FIRST EDITION

Printed in the United States of America.

A YOLLA BOLLY PRESS BOOK

The Living Kitchen was produced in association with the publisher at The Yolla Bolly Press, Covelo, California. Editorial and design staff: James and Carolyn Robertson, Diana Fairbanks, Joyca Cunnan, Barbara Youngblood, and Juliana Yoder.

The Sierra Club, founded in 1892 by John Muir, has devoted itself to the study and protection of the earth's scenic and ecological resources — mountains, wetlands, woodlands, wild shores and rivers, deserts and plains. Its publications are part of the nonprofit effort the club carries on as a public trust. There are more than 50 chapters coast to coast, in Canada, Hawaii, and Alaska. For information about how you may participate in the club's programs to enjoy and preserve wilderness and the quality of life, please address inquiries to Sierra Club, 530 Bush Street, San Francisco, California 94108.

LIBRARY OF CONGRESS CATALOGING IN PUBLICATION DATA

Cadwallader, Sharon.
The living kitchen.
(Sierra Club tools for today)
"A Yolla Bolly Press book."
Bibliography: p.
Includes index.
1. Food. 2. Cookery. 3. Kitchens. I. Title. II. Series.
TX353.C23 1983   641   82-10763
ISBN 0-87156-326-6

For Jeanne Wakatsuki Houston
and her wonderful, inspirational kitchen

Contents

The last decade in the United States has brought many humanizing changes in day-to-day living, with new attitudes toward health and hearth. The motivation for most of these shifts in lifestyle has been our fear that we are surrendering to the buttons and levers of an industrial society. We need to revive some of the acts and rituals of doing for ourselves in order to maintain more control over our lives. It is not that we renounce technology; we cannot all return to the simple life or go back to the land for total subsistence. Nor can we make for ourselves all the necessities for survival. We think of these changes as ways to find a balance between self-sufficiency and the reliance on machinery. This book is my attempt to create that balance, a harmony, in the modern kitchen.

The saga of the American kitchen has made an interesting cycle. In the early days the kitchen was the center of the home, the pulse of family life, and the family was the basic survival unit in the early colonies. The kitchen was referred to as the "common room," a kind of kitchen/living room, and no matter how many other rooms were added to the basic structure, the common room remained the center of the home. Cooking was done in and over the fireplace, which was very large because it was the only source of heat. Later, brick ovens for roasting and baking were built into the fireplace.

These large rooms were filled with family activity. The women did all their spinning, dyeing, sewing, weaving, and candlemaking in the warmth of the common room. Children played or studied there, and the baby's cradle remained near the hearth day and night. At the end of the day's work, the men gathered around the table to discuss local problems and politics. In the evening both young and old sat on benches in the warm corner of the hearth while the head of the household read from the Bible. It was not unusual for the master and mistress to sleep in the common room, and quite often the young children slept in a trundle bed which was stored under their parents' bed during the day. It was not until much later, in city houses, that food preparation was moved to a special room separate from the dining and entertaining area. Even then the kitchen continued to be a gathering spot for all the servants.

Prior to the advent of central heating, the kitchen, large or small, offered the necessary warmth to draw in the family during the chilly morning and evening hours. On the midwestern prairies, where fireplaces were rare because of the scarcity of wood, the kitchen stove, stoked with soft coal, was kept burning all day in the cold months while the doors to the other rooms were closed to prevent drafts. Consequently, everyone gathered in the kitchen. If the kitchen and dining area were one, there was often a separate summer kitchen with a kerosene stove, which did not emit heat like a wood-burning stove did. Or, in some instances, houses contained separate dining rooms, where the family could escape the heat of the cookstove during the hot months. The living room or parlor usually had a coal-burning heating stove, but such rooms were used only for company or special occasions.

As the years passed, especially in this century, the paring down of the kitchen's function continued until it reached an all-time low after World War II. The family's structure had altered too. Women were working outside the home, and the around-the-clock job cycle resulted in the disintegration of the family's dinner as a gathering point in the day. In addition, post-war food production introduced a new way of cooking and serving so that the kitchen became nothing but a place for heating and dispensing commercially prepared foods. Architecture, adapting to the changes in family life, created cubicle kitchens in which there was barely enough room for one person to work. Then the "den," in another part of the house, became the gathering place. Later the family room, adjacent to the kitchen, became the room where everyone ate and gathered, but the confusion of the noise from radio, then television, and the divergent schedules of family members were not conducive to family unity. The kitchen was a small and sterile spot where no one wanted to spend much time. Besides, the food industry had practically usurped the cook's role. (I wonder if the reliance on commercially prepared foods resulted in the lack of cooking skills seen in the second generation after the war and the subsequent increase in eating in restaurants.)

Fortunately, in the 1970s awareness of the poor quality

of American diets started a reversal of some of those post-war changes in the kitchen's image. New ideas about family roles and the emphasis on the mutual responsibility for raising children and preparing meals have had a positive effect on the family unit. And the general trend in architecture toward the informal and natural has affected kitchen design.

New concepts about food and eating, the earth, natural resources and energy, buildings and space, and human relationships are affecting all areas of living. The current trend toward living "whole" and "contributive" lives on a daily basis is helping to restore the kitchen to its original function — the center for nourishment, both physical and emotional.

This book is an attempt to help the modern American see the kitchen as that center. Chapter One describes current and accepted ideas about food value and cooking. Chapter Two suggests some ways of growing part of your own food. Chapter Three is about canning and preserving foods. Chapter Four has some ideas and sources for buying foods and for storing them properly. Chapter Five offers some design options for creating a more efficient kitchen. And the last chapter is all about personalizing the kitchen and transforming it into a gathering place for friends and family as well as a studio for preparing and serving food creatively.

Sharon Cadwallader
Santa Cruz, California
January, 1982

CHAPTER ONE
The Healthful Kitchen
NUTRITIVE VALUES OF FOOD

Grains & Flours

Meat & Alternate Protein

Vegetables & Fruits

Milk Products

Chapter One

The Healthful Kitchen

Americans have been concerned about various problems in the national diet for the better part of this century. As far back as 1906, Upton Sinclair published a novel entitled *The Jungle,* which exposed the substandard practices of the meat industry. Then in 1933 a book entitled *100,000 Guinea Pigs* shocked the nation when it revealed facts and figures about the extent of adulteration of both food and cosmetics. In the 1960s consumer advocates spoke out repeatedly against breakfast cereals, baby foods, and the excessive use of sugar and frequently criticized the government agencies that regulate the quality of processed foods. Certainly, therefore, interest in food and nutrition is not simply a product of the last decade as one may be quick to conclude. Yet, there is no question that in the past ten years there has been more dietary discussion and experimentation, more vocal indignation over the quality of commercial goods, more written protest against the operations of the American food industry, and more genuine interest in improving our cooking skills and eating habits than ever before. In fact, not since Captain John Smith ordered every Virginia family to grow corn for the survival of the colony has there been such collective determination to upgrade the American diet.

I remember the early seventies as being full of righteous anger over the extent to which chemically laden, overprocessed foods had invaded the American menu — a phenomenon that had been on the increase since World

War II. During those years that anger was directly responsible for some very revolutionary ideas about what we should and should not eat. Admittedly, there were many unsubstantiated theories about what is really good for the human body, but there was also enough genuine concern in all of us to encourage the food professionals — nutritionists, home economists, consumer advocates, and legislators — to investigate more carefully the food industry and the American diet.

Furthermore, the search for and research on what constitutes a good diet have also been influenced by the interest in gourmet and ethnic cooking. Taken at their healthful best, elegant and/or foreign dishes rely on fresh and unadulterated ingredients, guidelines that are compatible with those for natural food or vegetarian cooking.

Threats of global food shortages have forced food researchers to begin developing ways to process healthful foods creatively. Food products made from the protein-rich soybean, for example, have been developed as a substitute for meat proteins. Fortunately, we have reached a point where everyone who is genuinely interested in cooking agrees that the quality of ingredients and the care and creativity in food preparation are the fundamentals to a healthful diet.

Other major influences on our food habits are exercise, economy, and time. We Americans are going through an encouraging period of reevaluating our bodies. And thanks to the influence of medical research, which has connected poor diet and lack of exercise with ill health, many of us have incorporated a daily exercise program into our lives. Rising food prices, too, have shaped our eating patterns. The majority of Americans have to pay careful attention to what they include in the market basket since food prices are climbing so fast. This increase in the cost of food is a powerful argument against buying empty-calorie foods (processed foods with little nutritional value).

Personal time schedules also have an impact on our eating style. Most of us are pretty busy and now and then fall prey to quickie foods and eating in restaurants. However, most of us also recognize the arguments against those compromises — high cost, low quality, and the fact that a simple, well-planned menu actually competes timewise with going out to a restaurant or heating up a frozen dinner.

It's a good idea to incorporate the entire family in restructuring the function of your kitchen. One effective way to teach young people the value and limitation of your food dollar is to give them shopping and cooking responsibilities. This is especially important for working parents. If each child is given the responsibility to do the menu planning and shopping for a week at a time, and the preparation of at least one meal a day, chances are he or she will develop a much better understanding of the family's food budget. It also allows the child to see how difficult it is to be economical when buying prepared foods.

A family can organize its own personal recipe book too. Simply keep a record of what you cook for each evening meal, and its cost and preparation time. Enter this information with a date so younger members will be able to see changes in food prices and how they affect the type of meals you plan.

To begin to organize your kitchen so that you can prepare tasty, easy, healthful meals, I think it's helpful to re-examine what we have learned over these years. This chapter attempts to synthesize the new attitudes toward menu planning by redefining the four food groups and to show you how to use them according to your lifestyle and budget. Following is a list of terms which have received a lot of attention in the last ten years. Because some of these terms have been overworked to misunderstanding and confusion, I think it is a good idea to clarify them right here at the beginning.

Nutrients are the elements in foods that are essential to the building, upkeep, and repair of body tissue. "Nutrition" is the way in which each body uses nutrients. Although everyone needs the same nutrients to sustain a healthy life, the amounts needed will vary according to body type and lifestyle. It's important to know how foods affect us so that we can create diets that are personally beneficial.

Natural foods are those that have not been refined or adulterated by the food industry. By this I mean canned,

17

frozen, toasted, popped, precooked, enriched, preserved, flavored, sweetened, colored, spiced, cured, smoked, or the like. Some of this processing has little or no adverse effect on the nutrients in foods, while other techniques or additions remove or destroy many nutrients. In short, natural foods are those foods that are in their "natural" or "basic" form.

Organic foods are those that are raised without artificial treatment or feeding. This term includes animals that are allowed to scratch or graze freely and are not fed chemicals to stimulate growth. Many organic foods cost more because they require more physical space or maturation time, and many large-scale farmers maintain that they are unable to practice organic farming methods without pushing the cost onto the consumer, even though this contention is disputed in agricultural and food circles. However, if a cow must be fed twenty-one pounds of grain to produce one pound of meat for human consumption, we could surely decrease our food costs if our diets were higher in vegetable protein than in meat protein. If this substitution were the trend, I think all of us would have a little more money to spend for organically grown foods.

Processed foods are those items that have been through a treatment; they have been refined or adulterated before they reach the consumer. Although types of treatments vary from simple to complex, some processing is necessary for storage and distribution. Strictly speaking, processed foods are the opposite of natural foods.

Preservatives and additives can be natural substances or chemicals that are added to foods to preserve freshness and augment taste and color. There is still a great deal of controversy over the harm or value of preservatives and additives in food. Some appear to be harmless (the citric acid that is often added to fruit juices); others are obviously detrimental to certain health conditions (sodium-laced foods cannot be recommended for people on low-sodium diets). Many have yet to be proven harmless.

A vegetarian (or vegan) is one who, strictly or purely speaking, eats only foods of plant origin and eats no foods of animal origin. A lacto-vegetarian is one who includes dairy products in his or her diet.

18

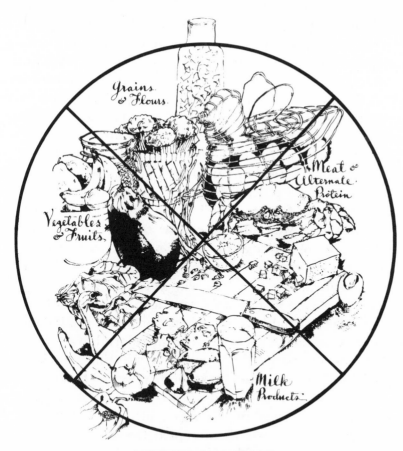

THE FOUR FOOD GROUPS

Except for people who are on special diets for particular medical problems, the following guide for a daily menu can apply to anyone. As I already mentioned, everyone needs the same nutrients throughout life, but the amounts needed will differ according to our age, sex, physical activity, and body type. People who are under stress, physical or emotional, do well to increase their vitamin B and protein intake; pregnant women and growing children must take care to get sufficient amounts of vitamins A and D and calcium. People who are recovering from illnesses should follow a consistently balanced diet, while the elderly are usually instructed to watch their intake of fatty foods. Also, many of us have allergies and must replace the problem foods with alternate or supplementary sources of nutrients. There is no question that we must become aware of our particular dietary needs to remain healthy.

19

It is also important to remember when planning an adequate diet that no one food provides all the nutrients necessary for good health. We need a *variety* of foods each day. Unfortunately, this can be a real problem to the American consumer, who, although faced with a monumental variety of foods in today's supermarkets, still is seeing simply many processing variations on the same theme. As a rule of thumb, it's best to look for the "natural" or "basic" food when following the food groups, rather than the processed, ready-mixed competitor. In most instances food costs will be less if you do your own preparation. (After all, you can be certain the food industry is going to charge you for being your cook.) And in all cases the nutrient value will be greater in a diet of basic foods that you prepare with your own recipes.

It has been a tradition in American grammar school curricula to include a little information about good foods for growing children. I remember the colorful food wheel that was supposed to be a guide for selecting the right foods each day. It must have been effective because it stuck in my mind, and I can still see the drawings of milk bottles, bread loaves, meat chops, fruits, and vegetables.

These foods are still the accepted foods for obtaining necessary nutrients. The United States Department of Agriculture and most nutrition scientists agree that our diets should be made up of foods from four basic food groups. However, there have been improvements on these basic categories — such as adding alternate plant protein to the old textbook protein group of meat, fish, poultry, and eggs, and adding yogurt to the milk group. The loaf of white bread in the bread and cereal group has been replaced and now includes whole grains and whole-grain baked products. This update of the food groups is a result of the changes in our thinking about food during these past few years. Broadly speaking here is what these foods provide in our diets.

Meat and alternate protein are necessary for the development and repair of all body tissues. These foods also offer iron and B vitamins to our diets.

Vegetables and fruits give us most of our vitamin C and a very large portion of our vitamin A and minerals. Vitamin C is needed for maintenance of body tissues, especially the mucous membranes and gums. Vitamin A is necessary for nourishing healthy skin and normal vision. Minerals help provide body strength and energy and are important for maintaining a healthy nervous system.

Milk products such as whole and skim milk, buttermilk, yogurt, and cheese are important sources of calcium. Calcium is the mineral that is vital to the development of bones and teeth. Milk products also provide protein, vitamin A, and vitamin B_2 (riboflavin). Buttermilk, yogurt, acidophilus milk, and kefir provide healthy intestinal bacteria to aid digestion.

Grains and flours provide protein, iron, B vitamins, and minerals and are especially effective when balanced with other protein foods.

Fats, oils, and sweets are not included in the four groups because they are not part of every diet. In fact, fats and sweets, especially, are recommended only in very small amounts in a healthy diet. Both animal and vegetable protein contain fat and oil, and vegetables and fruits are good sources of natural sugars. While water is not considered a food, it is essential to the digestion and elimination of food and for the transportation of nutrients through the body as well as for maintaining body fluids. A reasonable amount of water, other than that found in beverages, should be included in everyone's daily diet.

USING THE FOOD GROUPS

We must be flexible when using the food groups as a guide. As I continue to emphasize, the amounts of nutrients needed differ — nearly as much as our personalities. Calorie requirements also vary according to our ages and the energy we expire each day. Tastes, too, must be taken into consideration. If a food is not palatable, as milk and eggs sometimes aren't to children, these same foods can be used in baking instead. One nice thing about this planet is that is provides us with so many basic food choices.

MEAT AND ALTERNATE PROTEIN GROUP

Foods included: Beef, pork, lamb, veal, poultry, seafood, eggs, dry beans, dry peas, lentils, nuts, and seeds.

21

This group also includes the many foods being developed from the protein-rich soybean, such as soybean curd and tofu.

Amount recommended: Generally speaking, a person getting a normal amount of activity should have an intake of 0.42 grams of protein for each pound of body weight each day. To determine the approximate number of grams of protein you need every day, divide your body weight by two. A good daily menu would include two servings of two or three ounces of complete protein foods. Complete protein includes alternate protein foods that are balanced with each other to complete the amino acid balance. For example, if you eat rice and legumes at the same meal, you would be eating complete, balanced protein. Two more examples of plant foods combining to form complete protein are wheat and beans, and peanuts and sunflower seeds. An excellent reference for learning to balance alternate, or plant, protein is Frances Lappe Moore's book *Diet for a Small Planet*.

Caution: Meat and meat products, such as bacon, salt pork, and canned and packaged luncheon meat, should be low priorities in a healthy, economical diet. They are expensive in relation to the protein dollar, and they are high in sodium and chemical additives. Eggs, while a good economical protein source, should be limited in a diet correcting high cholesterol.

Economy: I think the most sensible and economic program for obtaining adequate protein is to include a recipe of alternate (vegetarian) protein as one of your daily servings. Or make every other day vegetarian. After preparing a few vegetarian protein recipes, you will find it easy to balance different plant proteins so that you can create your own recipes. One serving of either of the two following recipes meets almost one-half of our daily protein needs.

Mixed Vegetables and Tofu with Brown Rice

1 pound tofu (soybean curd)
1/2 cup soy sauce
1/4 teaspoon powdered ginger
1/4 teaspoon powdered cumin

22

1/8 teaspoon hot pepper sauce
1 tablespoon apple-cider vinegar
3 tablespoons sesame seeds
3 tablespoons oil
1 cup chopped green onions
1 cup chopped celery
3 cloves garlic, mashed or minced
2 cups chopped summer squash
1 bunch spinach, chopped
salt
2-1/2 cups brown rice, cooked

Drain tofu and cut into 1/2-inch cubes. Mix together soy sauce, ginger, cumin, hot pepper sauce, and vinegar. Pour over tofu, coating it well. In frying pan toast sesame seeds over low heat until golden brown, then remove from pan and set aside. Heat oil in pan and saute onions, celery, and garlic until slightly softened, then add squash and spinach and cook and stir until tender. Remove tofu from marinade with slotted spoon and add to vegetable mixture. Add enough marinade to taste and stir and cook until tofu is well heated. Salt lightly to taste. Serve over brown rice topped with toasted sesame seeds. Serves 6.

Cheesed Eggs and Tomatoes on Wheat Toast

4 tablespoons butter or margarine
4 tablespoons unbleached flour
3 cups whole milk
2 cups grated sharp cheddar cheese
1/2 teaspoon dry mustard
salt
6 large eggs
2 large tomatoes, cored and sliced in thirds
6 slices whole wheat bread, toasted
2 tablespoons toasted sesame seeds (optional)

In a saucepan melt butter or margarine and stir in flour to make a roux. Add milk, cheese, and mustard and stir over a low heat until thickened. Salt to taste. Keep warm. Poach eggs in water while broiling tomatoes lightly (just to heat). On each piece of toast place one slice of tomato and one poached egg. Then pour cheese sauce over these and top with toasted sesame seeds if desired. Serves 6.

Foods included: All fruits and vegetables in all forms — fresh, frozen, canned, dried, and juiced. The nutrient emphasis in this group is vitamins A and C and minerals. Good sources of vitamin A are dark green leafy vegetables, yellow vegetables, broccoli, apricots, mangoes, persimmons, and all of the winter squash. Good sources of vitamin C are grapefruit, oranges, cantaloupes, guavas, mangoes, papayas, strawberries, brussels sprouts, broccoli, peppers, currants, Jerusalem artichokes, and tomatoes. Good mineral sources are green leafy vegetables, tomatoes, celery, rutabagas, winter squash, eggplant, potatoes, peas, brussels sprouts, all dried fruits, melons, citrus fruits, and bananas.

Amount recommended: Everyone should try to have at least one serving of a good vitamin C source and one of a good vitamin A source every day. It is also suggested that everyone have two or three other servings of vegetables or fruits each day. A serving should be at least one-half cup of a diced fruit or cooked vegetable; six to eight ounces of juice; or one whole orange, apple, banana, or potato; or one-half grapefruit or cantaloupe.

Caution: Whenever possible, use fresh produce. Choose unblemished fruits and vegetables, ripe, but not oversoft, firm, but not green. Steaming vegetables above water preserves nutrients and is a good low-calorie method of preparation if you add just a little lemon or vinegar to the cooked vegetables. If you cook vegetables in oil or water, be careful not to overcook them.

Economy: Buy seasonal produce whenever possible; it will be fresher and cheaper. Most fruits and vegetables are versatile, and it's wise to keep a substantial number of recipes on hand to utilize a windfall or abundant supply of one fruit or vegetable. My favorite example is summer squash, which comes in spades, especially since there are so many home gardens now. Fortunately, all summer squash can be used in a wide variety of recipes (see recipes following), but this is also true of winter apples and summer fruits. We need to think of everything from hot dishes to desserts for both fruits and vegetables.

Sweet Zucchini Bread

1-3/4 cups unbleached flour
1/4 cup raw wheat germ
3 teaspoons baking powder
1 teaspoon salt
1/2 teaspoon cinnamon
1 egg
1/2 cup butter or margarine, melted
1/2 cup honey
1 teaspoon vanilla
1 cup grated zucchini
1/2 cup chopped nuts

Mix together dry ingredients. Beat egg with butter, honey, and vanilla. Fold in zucchini and nuts. Mix with dry ingredients just until well moistened. Turn into a lightly greased 9-by-5-inch loaf pan and bake in preheated 350° oven for 45 to 50 minutes. Cool before serving. Makes one loaf.

Zucchini Protein Salad

3 cups grated raw zucchini
2 hard-boiled eggs, grated
2 cups finely shredded cabbage
1 cup grated Swiss cheese
1 small onion, halved and thinly sliced
1 teaspoon dill weed
vinaigrette dressing
salt and pepper

Press excess liquid from zucchini and toss with eggs, cabbage, cheese, onion, and dill weed. Dress lightly with a vinaigrette dressing and salt and pepper to taste. Serves 4 to 5.

Zucchini and Mushroom Pizza

3 cups grated raw zucchini
3 eggs, well beaten
1/3 cup unbleached flour
1/4 teaspoon salt
2 cups grated mozzarella cheese
2 cups fresh, sliced mushrooms
2/3 cup minced green onions
1/2 cup minced Italian pickled peppers
1 teaspoon each dried oregano and basil
2 large ripe tomatoes

Press excess liquid from zucchini and mix with eggs, flour, and salt. Spread in a lightly greased 9-by-13-inch baking pan or cookie sheet with lip.

25

Bake in a preheated 450° oven for 7 or 8 minutes. Remove from oven and reduce temperature to 350°. Cover zucchini crust with cheese, then arrange mushrooms, onions, and peppers evenly on top of cheese. Sprinkle with oregano and basil and top with tomato slices. Bake until base is well set and cheese is bubbly (about 20 minutes). Serves 4 to 6.

MILK GROUP

Foods included: Milk, whole, low fat, skim, evaporated, dry; buttermilk; yogurt; kefir; all cheeses, natural or processed; cottage cheese; ricotta cheese; ice cream.

Amounts recommended daily:

Children under 9	2 or 3 glasses
Children 9 to 12	3 or more glasses
Teenagers	4 or more glasses
Pregnant women	3 or more glasses
Nursing mothers	4 or more glasses
Adults	2 or more glasses

In case of milk allergies, other calcium-rich foods should be substituted in the diet each day. Good sources are shellfish, blackstrap molasses, and green, leafy vegetables. Too, calcium supplements are available, but they should be balanced with magnesium to be properly absorbed (two parts calcium to one part magnesium).

Milk products can satisfy the daily need for fresh milk in the following proportions:

Ricotta cheese	1/2 cup to 1 cup milk
Yogurt, cottage cheese	1/2 cup to 1 cup milk
Natural cheese, 1-inch square	1/2 cup milk

Caution: Processed cheeses and cheese foods are not recommended as rich calcium sources in the milk group, and they are expensive and contain chemical additives. People who are on low-sodium diets should eat sparingly of all cheeses, including cottage and ricotta cheese, as they all contain a hearty amount of salt. However, yogurt cheese, to which no salt is added, is easy to make (see recipe on page 27).

Economy: Milk, especially dry milk, and cottage and ricotta cheese are good, inexpensive sources of protein. Natural cheeses, although seemingly expensive in bulk, are also good protein sources as it takes only a little in a recipe to balance a plant protein. On the other hand, yogurt and, certainly, ice cream are more expensive sources of protein in terms of the amount of protein per dollar spent. Yogurt should be regarded as a digestive aid and as a low-calorie substitute for sour cream. (Of course, making your own yogurt is a considerable savings.)

Yogurt Cheese

Line a large, deep bowl with several layers of cheesecloth. Scoop into the cheesecloth 2 pints of unflavored whole-milk yogurt and tie the ends together with a string, then tie the bundle to the middle of a large knife or spoon and lay the utensil across the top of the bowl, resting it on the edges so the bottom of the cheesecloth clears the bottom of the bowl. Put the bowl in the refrigerator for 5 hours while the whey drains off. Transfer the curds or cheese to a container and mix with herbs and spices such as garlic, minced onion, dill, mint, curry, and cumin. Spread the cheese on crackers or bread. Save the whey to drink or to use in soups.

Dry Milk Custard

1 scant cup dry milk powder
3-1/2 cups water
6 whole eggs
1/2 cup honey
2 teaspoons vanilla
dash of salt
Put all ingredients in a blender and blend well. Pour into an oven-proof dish or individual custard molds and place in a shallow pan of hot water. (Water should come up to the middle of the dish or dishes.) Place in a preheated 350° oven for 45 minutes to 1-1/2 hours, depending on the dishes. A thin knife should come out almost clean when inserted in the middle. Do not overcook; custards continue to cook a little after they have been removed from the oven. Serves 6.

Foods included: All whole and cracked grains, grits, grain meal, whole-grain flours, and all related food products — yeast breads, quick breads, crackers, hot and cold cereals, and pasta.

Amounts recommended: For children and teenagers, four to five servings a day are suggested; for adults, three servings. One serving is equivalent to one slice of bread or one muffin; one ounce dry cereal; one-half cup cooked cereal, grain, or pasta.

Caution: To obtain maximum nutrients from this food group it's suggested that whole-grain bread products be used, rather than foods made from refined flours. Wheat gluten (protein) allergies can be compensated for by using other grains, and there are some gluten-free bread products on the market.

Economy: If you buy substantial amounts of whole-grain flours, it is generally cheaper to make your own bread. Quick breads and muffins are easy recipes for a busy schedule, and it's an economical snap to make your own healthy baking mixes. You will save money and your health if you avoid buying pasta or grain mixes. Packaged cold cereals are expensive for the amount of nutrients they offer and are very easy to make at home (see recipes on the following pages).

Multigrain Muffins

1 cup whole wheat flour
1/3 cup yellow cornmeal
1/3 cup brown rice flour
1/3 cup soy flour
1/2 teaspoon baking soda
1 teaspoon baking powder
1 scant teaspoon salt
3 tablespoons brown sugar
2 eggs
1 cup buttermilk or sour milk
1/4 cup oil
Mix together dry ingredients. Beat eggs with buttermilk, or sour milk, and oil. Combine all ingredients just enough to moisten. Spoon into 12 lightly greased muffin cups and bake in a 400° oven for about 15 minutes, or until nicely golden.

---

6 cups whole wheat flour
1 cup raw wheat germ
1 cup brown rice, soy, or millet flour
1/2 cup flaked bran (not bran flakes cereal)
1 cup dry milk powder (for extra protein)
3-1/2 tablespoons baking powder
3 teaspoons salt

Whole-Grain Baking Mix

Combine all ingredients well. Store in a tightly covered container in the refrigerator and use as needed.

2 cups Whole-Grain Baking Mix
2 eggs
1 cup milk
1/4 cup oil
2 tablespoons honey

Muffins

Put baking mix in a bowl. Beat eggs with milk, oil, and honey and stir into mix only until all ingredients are moistened. Spoon into 12 lightly greased muffin cups and bake in a 400° oven for about 20 minutes, or until golden.

2 cups Whole-Grain Baking Mix
2 eggs, separated
1-2/3 cups milk
3 tablespoons oil
2 tablespoons honey

Pancakes

Put baking mix in a bowl. Beat egg yolks with milk, oil, and honey and stir into mix just until all ingredients are moistened. Beat egg whites stiff and fold into batter. Spoon onto a hot, greased griddle and turn once when surface bubbles break. Makes 18 to 20 pancakes. Add more milk for thinner pancakes.

Follow the directions for pancakes, but increase the oil to 4 tablespoons. Spoon onto a hot waffle iron. Makes about 6 average waffles.

Waffles

Cold or Hot Swiss Cereal

3 cups quick-cooking oats
1 cup raw wheat germ
2 cups rolled wheat (also called wheat flakes)
1-1/2 cups chopped nuts (pecans, almonds, walnuts, or a mixture)
1 cup raisins
1 cup chopped dried fruit (apricots, dates, figs)

Mix all ingredients and store in a tightly covered container in the refrigerator. Makes about 2 quarts.

Serve cold with milk or mix one cup cereal to one cup water with a dash of salt and cook over medium heat for about 5 minutes.

Easy Granola

5 cups rolled oats
1 cup shelled sunflower seeds
1-1/2 cups raw wheat germ
2-1/2 cups unsweetened shredded coconut
1 cup chopped walnuts
1/2 teaspoon salt
3/4 cup honey
1/2 cup light oil
2 teaspoons vanilla
1 cup raisins

Combine oats, seeds, wheat germ, coconut, and walnuts. Stir in salt. In a saucepan heat honey, oil, and vanilla and pour over dry mixture. Spread in a shallow baking pan (or two) about 1/2 inch deep and bake in a 350° oven for 1/2 hour, or until lightly browned. Stir frequently so edges do not brown first. Cool and store in the refrigerator in a tightly covered container. Makes about 3 quarts.

The Book of Tofu, revised edition. William Shurtleff **Suggested Reading**
and Akiko Aoyagi. Ballantine Books.

Diet for a Small Planet. Frances Lappe Moore. Ballantine Books.

Laurel's Kitchen. Laurel Robertson, Carol Flinders, and Bronwen Godfrey. Bantam Books.

Tofu Goes West. Gary Landgreb. Fress Press.

The Vegetarian Epicure (2 vols.). Anna Thomas. Vintage Books.

Whole Earth Cooking for the 80's. Sharon Cadwallader. St. Martin's Press.

CHAPTER TWO
The Kitchen Garden
RAISING SOME OF YOUR OWN FOOD

Chapter Two

The Kitchen Garden

This chapter is for the closet gardener. And although many of us have only limited space for plot gardening, it is still possible to grow a few vegetables and some of the herbs that flavor them with a minimum of time, effort, and garden area.

As you try to make your kitchen a more integral part of your lifestyle, growing a few foods in and around your home will keep your family aware of the source and flow of food and nourishment. Gardening is an especially nice group project; it's a good way to teach children about the food cycle and to help them understand the care that is put into raising food. Also, home gardening teaches all of us to be more conscious of the basic foods for good health, and how to care for fresh foods.

If you don't have room for a traditional garden plot, consider planting in narrow beds or borders around your house or patio. In one of the houses where my parents lived, my mother grew greens and tomatoes in a slender strip of earth under the kitchen window — a far more useful planting than decorative hedges or flowers that aren't even visible from inside. Container gardening, too, is an easy and inexpensive method of growing enough greens for salads or soups, or enough herbs to last through the coming year. Also, container gardening is a way of obtaining some of the high-ticket foods such as sorrel or shallots or international ingredients such as endive, cilantro, or fennel. Where I am living now I can garden only in containers, but I still manage to grow some of my summer vegetables, and I always maintain a limited, but year-round, herb garden.

Community garden plots are available in many cities and towns. There are some very nice ones in my little town, and in my parents' retirement community, where the residences are condominiums, there is a substantial area outside of town for garden plots. Here some remarkable gardens are flourishing, and each year my father grows a major portion of the vegetables they eat. The result is two very spry senior citizens.

To make your garden a successful and fruitful part of your "whole kitchen," plant foods that do well in your area. The yield will be greater and the plants stronger, and it will also give your family a sense of what *is* the natural diet of your particular geographical area. We are fortunate that transportation and storage have given us access to foods from other sections of the world, but that same good fortune allows us to forget about regional diversity and how it affects our diet. After all, what we call "ethnic cooking" is simply a diet that is planned around what was, and is, available in a particular section of the earth.

PLOT GARDENING

Determine first of all the size of your plot. In many cases, especially in the inner city, your space will be small. If so, here are a few ideas that may help you take advantage of whatever area you do have.

1. Start your seedlings indoors if possible. This is wise in extremely seasonal areas, and if you want to have several crops in a season.

2. Plant vegetables that continue to produce as you harvest them — leafy vegetables, broccoli, beans, peas, winter and summer squash (if you have room), and tomatoes.

3. Plant "upwards." Besides peas and beans, you can stake and support squash, tomatoes, and cucumbers.

4. Make narrow avenues for walking. You can plant two rows of vegetables to every single walkway to make the best use of space.

5. Plant tall vegetables — vines and corn, for example, on the north side so your growing space won't be lost to shade.

Soil must be neither too acid (sour) nor too alkaline (sweet) to grow a large variety of vegetables. You can determine the type of soil you have by testing it with litmus paper, which is available in nurseries. Make a solution of half soil and half water, then dip in the paper. Compare it with the color chart that comes with the package. Since most plants do well in a slightly acidic soil, a pH of 6.5 is a good goal for the summer gardener. As a rule of thumb, dry climates produce more alkaline soils, while wet areas tend to have acidic soils.

I remember once trying to garden in the redwood area of California without first preparing the soil. The soil's high acidity cost me most of the first year's crop. If I had added even a little dolomite limestone to neutralize it some, I might have doubled my yield. If your soil tests acid, consult your nursery for the amount of limestone needed for your garden size.

If, on the other hand, your soil is too alkaline, water it heavily to leach out the salts, then add sulphur to acidify it. Again, consult a nursery on the amount of sulphur needed per square foot. These preparations take from weeks to months to alter the soil, so this should be one of the first steps in your garden project. Then, when the soil tests acid to neutral, it's time to compost.

Composting is recommended for all gardens, large or small. Combine kitchen garbage with cuttings — grass, leaves, and weeds — and in time you will have a rich lunch for your garden. Adding a little nitrogen is recommended, too, as watering quickly leaches nitrogen from soil, even very good soil. Consult your local nursery for available nitrogen-rich manures.

Place your compost pile in a little-used area of your garden, preferably in a shady spot so the pile(s) will not dry out too fast. If your acreage is small, it's smart to compost in closed bins to keep away flies and animals. Large plastic garbage containers work well as compost containers.

Compost in layers, dry and moist, and place a layer of sawdust on the bottom and on the top to cover any ripe compost. Water the pile lightly as it should be kept moist (but not soggy). Let it sit for a couple of days, then turn it by gathering the sides into the middle and turning the top to the bottom. The turning provides oxygen throughout the pile and distributes the decomposing heat of the center to kill off any fly eggs and larvae. The center should heat up to 160° after a couple of days. Then, as it is turned, it cools down until it is dry. Too much nitrogen will give off an ammonia odor; if that happens, you should add more leaves or sawdust to the pile. Too little nitrogen will inhibit the heating and decomposition process, and in that case you should add a little blood meal. A good decomposing compost can be added to garden soil in a week, but you should not plant the area for two or three weeks afterward. However, continue to work the soil each day to mix it well and keep it light. Dry compost can be used as mulch or as fertilizer during the growing period of your plants, providing it has finished its decomposition process. It should not be worked in around plants until it is dry; the high nitrogen content can damage the plants.

There is a good book called *Hunger Signs in Crops* that will help you learn to recognize mineral deficiencies in your plants, and how to feed them accordingly. It is published by David McKay Company and edited by Howard B. Sprague.

PLANNING YOUR PLOT

What you choose to grow in your garden depends both on the size of your plot and your personal preference. Even if your garden area is small, it's nice to have a few root vegetables. If you start early enough in the season and start seeds indoors, you can replant root vegetables once, or even twice, before the ground gets too cold for planting.

For your garden, choose an area that gets maximum sun and is not near trees, to avoid their roots as well as their shade. Decide what you want to raise, and plan your garden on paper. Start your seedlings indoors as you begin to cultivate the soil. If, for example, you have an area approximately six feet by eighteen feet and you want a good variety of vegetables, you could use the garden layout illustrated here.

Garden Layouts

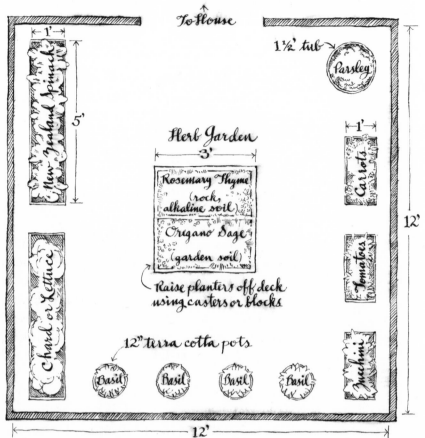

To House

1½' tub — Parsley

Herb Garden
3'

Rosemary Thyme
(rock,
alkaline soil)

Oregano Sage
(garden soil)

Raise planters off deck
using casters or blocks

12" terra cotta pots

Basil   Basil   Basil   Basil

1'
New Zealand Spinach

5'

Chard or Lettuce

1'
Carrots

Tomatoes

Zucchini

12'

12'

SUMMER DECK GARDEN IN PLANTER BOXES; SOUTHERN EXPOSURE

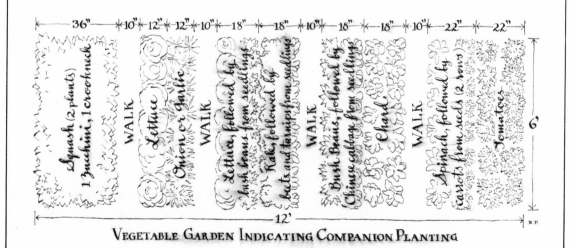

36" 10" 12" 12" 10" 18" 18" 10" 18" 18" 10" 22" 22"

Squash (2 plants)
1 Zucchini, 1 crookneck

WALK

Lettuce

Onion or Garlic

WALK

Lettuce, followed by
bush beans from seedlings

Kale, followed by
beets and turnips from seedlings

WALK

Bush Beans, followed by
Chinese cabbage from seedlings

Chard

WALK

Spinach, followed by
carrots from seeds (2 rows)

Tomatoes

6'

12'

VEGETABLE GARDEN INDICATING COMPANION PLANTING

In addition, herbs could be planted around the edge or in pots or planters. (Herbs generally prefer a sweet soil and good drainage.) This is just a suggestion, there are many layout possibilities; you may favor other vegetables. This size plot will feed a small family well if production is good.

Family-related crops (cabbage and broccoli, squash and cucumbers, for example) should be planted in different areas each season because they are subject to the same blights and pests.

STARTING PLANTS INDOORS

There are several reasons for starting your garden indoors. First of all, it's one way to get an early start on a garden in cold areas. Then, of course, it's a way of staggering crops in a small garden space. And, finally, you are less likely to lose seedlings to birds and pests.

If you are planning to start some seeds in the house, here are some suggestions I think are important.

1. Use prepared soils. They do very well for seedlings and are easier than combining soil substances for a planter. Or, if your garden soil is already in good shape, use one-third soil, one-third peat moss, and one-third sand. The latter two can be purchased at a nursery. Beach sand is too salty.

2. Use milk cartons (cut into cubes) or cottage cheese cartons (with drainage holes cut into the bottoms) for planting seeds indoors. Or you can use peat containers, which can be transplanted directly into the earth.

3. Set the soil-filled containers in a tray (aluminum freezer containers are good). Pack the soil gently and pour water into the containers; there should be a little water in the bottom of the tray. Make depressions in the soil, about an inch apart, with your fingers and drop in a couple of seeds; sprinkle a little sand over the top to keep out the light, but do not bury the seeds.

4. Keep seeds damp, not soaked, while germinating. A spray bottle is good for this.

5. Keep the container near light, and when the leaves appear, thin out the weakest seedlings. Snip off with scissors; do not pull them up. They are ready to transplant when their second leaves appear.

40

Container gardening is perfect for the inner-city dweller who has a little space on a deck or on a sunny porch or rooftop. If you have limited sun, you would do well to raise leafy vegetables such as spinach, chard, kale, and lettuce as well as peas and pole beans. Parsley does very well in shaded areas; and if you have a small sunny area, try tomatoes. All these vegetables continue to produce if they are picked regularly during their growing period, and so they offer good crop yields for their space. And as I mentioned at the beginning of this chapter, specialty foods are good candidates for container gardens.

There are many types of commercial containers for planter gardens, and most nurseries and hardware stores carry a large variety. I prefer to make redwood planters because they are durable, pleasantly rough-hewn, and easy to make. Narrow planters have two properties to consider: they are easy to build, and they are not heavy and cumbersome to move about. The design of the planters illustrated here is simple, and the planters are extremely easy to assemble, even if you have very few tools. I made mine and have been using them for ten years.

There are a number of soil suspensions you can use in planter gardens. A solution easy to obtain is a good outdoor potting soil recommended by your local nursery. Or, if you have a good finished compost, you can mix it half and half with garden soil, then add a little sand. If you have very good garden soil available, you can lessen the soil weight in the containers by using one-half garden soil, one-fourth vermiculite, and one-fourth perlite. In most instances, especially if you are using a commercial mix, it's wise to use a little fertilizer (such as fish emulsion) periodically during the growing period. Again, I emphasize that you should learn to recognize plant deficiencies.

If you are making up your own soil composition, use an old tub (you may have to make several batches to fill a planter), moistening the soil as you mix it to keep down the dust and to settle it.

Drainage is a crucial factor for the planter garden, and casters are a good addition to the redwood planter. Re-

Planter Box Construction

FIVE-FOOT PLANTER BOX

Materials needed:
- 3 pieces rough-sawn redwood, each 6 feet x 12 inches x 1 inch
- 1 pound 6d galvanized nails
- 10-point hand saw
- hammer

① Cut lumber as shown.

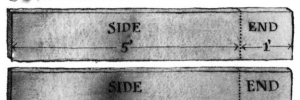

| SIDE 5' | END 1' |

| SIDE 5' | END 1' |

| BOTTOM 4'10" | BOTTOM BRACES 14" |

② Cut three 1-inch drainage notches on each side of the 4-foot 10-inch piece. Avoid knots.

CENTER — 1' / 1'

TWO-FOOT PLANTER BOX

Materials needed:
- 1 piece rough-sawn redwood, 8 feet x 12 inches x 1 inch
- ½ pound galvanized nails
- 10-point hand saw
- hammer

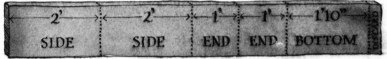

| 2' SIDE | 2' SIDE | 1' END | 1' END | 1'10" BOTTOM |

Notch bottom and follow the same procedure as for the larger planter box. Use casters or braces for drainage.

③ Square off one end piece to bottom piece and pound in three nails.

④ Attach side piece to end and bottom. Continue with other end and final side.

⑤ Nail 14-inch strips underneath to brace and elevate for drainage (or attach casters). Don't nail over notches.

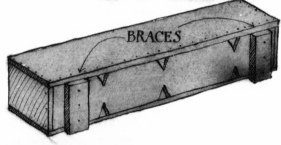

BRACES

B. P.

member that good soil does not drain like a sieve. Even so, if you are worried about water draining onto a balcony or rooftop, you can cut up plastic or dairy cartons and set them under the drainage holes.

PLANTING AND HARVESTING VEGETABLES

The following vegetables and herbs are most commonly found in home gardens all over the country. Information about growing additional regional foods can be obtained from the books in the suggested reading list at the end of the chapter.

Artichokes. Planting time varies according to geography, so it's best to consult a seed catalog in your area. Plant in trenches six to eight inches deep with a one-inch lining of mulch or loose fertilized soil. Mulch plants when they are four to five inches tall to keep them moist. After plants reach eight to nine inches in height, cut away all but a few suckers, using the suckers to make still another row. Fertilize once during the growing season and again after harvest. Cut the plants back to the ground in the fall. To harvest, cut off choke with one inch of stem when it is about the size of an orange. For freezing, use smaller chokes.

Asparagus. Because you must wait four years to pick asparagus grown from seed, you are wise to buy roots that already have a two- to three-year start. Plants will produce for up to ten or twelve years, and volunteer seedlings will replenish your crop each year. Select rust-resistant varieties and plant in early spring. Plant in ten-inch-deep trenches that are four to five inches apart. Soil should be about one-fourth to one-third sand, and trenches should have an inch or so of compost or dried manure on the bottom. Place plants eighteen inches apart and cover with three inches of soil. As plants grow, fill in the trench. Fertilize early with a little compost, working it into the soil and around the plant. Just as the spears begin to develop, work in one-half ounce of nitrate of soda around each plant. Transplant seedlings to a new row in late August or early spring. Asparagus beds should be picked faithfully after the fourth year and cut close to the ground once they are five to six inches tall. If the spears grow too high, they will become ferns, producing no more asparagus that season. The crop will slow after six weeks and then reappear the following year. After six weeks, let ferns grow.

Beans. Both wax and green beans come in bush and pole varieties, and if you have room, you can grow both to insure a long production period. Bush beans mature in seven to eight weeks. The pole varieties take a couple of weeks longer to mature, but if they are well staked, they have a long producing period. Plant both pole and bush beans as soon as the weather turns warm. Bush beans should be planted in fine soil three inches apart and one inch deep. When the seedlings are about three inches high, the plants should be thinned to five inches apart. Pole and lima beans like a little compost as they blossom. Bush beans generally do fine without attention as long as the soil is good. Marigolds planted between and around beans tend to keep off beetles. Snap beans should be picked continually to insure a long production period. Pick when they are anywhere from three to six inches in length and cook them immediately. Wait until wax beans are bright yellow before picking, and any shell bean is ready when it begins to round.

Beets. You can get two nice crops of beets if you start in early spring. Sow seeds in foot-wide furrows, no more than three seeds to one inch. They should be covered with one-half to one inch of good garden loam (not too sandy). When young greens are ready for picking, thin plants to stand at least two inches apart, and harvest if they become crowded. You can harvest the greens early on and continue to remove them as long as enough leaves are left on the plant for its nourishment. Remove beets before they get too large; generally they are best when they are about two to three inches in diameter. Larger beets are often fibrous. Beets can be stored in damp sand for from several weeks to a month.

Broccoli. Broccoli seeds should be planted in early spring when the ground is workable. One package of seeds will yield two dozen plants and requires about fifty feet of furrow, so adapt according to your plot size and shape. Seeds should be about one inch deep, covered with about one inch of soil, and tamped. Thin plants to eighteen inches apart when the seedlings reach three to four inches in height. A little fertilizer should be worked into the soil just before the heads appear. In cooler areas it's also possible to start seedlings indoors and transplant them when they are three inches high. Harvest broccoli when the florets have not yet separated and when each head is about three inches across. Cut with five to six inches of stem to promote growth of side shoots.

Cabbage. There are many varieties of cabbage, and all can be sown early in the spring when the ground is workable. (All but the Chinese, or Napa, varieties can be started indoors.) Plant as you would broccoli and cut the heads from the stem when they are solid. Discard or compost remaining plant to keep garden tidy. Onions planted around and between cabbage plants deter pests.

Carrots. Carrots can be planted from early spring to early summer; don't be discouraged by their slow germination. Sow in one-foot-wide trenches in finely worked soil. Cover firmly with one-half inch of soil and thin first when ferns are close to four inches tall, then again as they get taller. Carrots can be left in the ground until a frost, then stored in damp sand.

Cauliflower. Follow directions for planting broccoli, but as the heads develop, the leaves should be tied over them to improve their flavor and to keep them white. They will be ready to harvest about three weeks after the heads begin to form. Cut the heads from the plants and treat the remaining plant parts as you would cabbage. Or if you want to store cauliflower, remove the entire plant and hang it, inverted, in a cool, dark area. It will keep several weeks.

Chard. Plant as early in the spring as the ground can be worked. Sprinkle seeds in two-inch-deep furrows and cover tightly with one-half inch of good soil. Thin to three to four inches apart when plants are three inches high, and then again as they grow. Eat thinnings and harvest outer leaves first. Never strip the entire plant.

Sweet corn. Corn plantings can be staggered. Look on packages for early to late varieties. Plant in short rows so the corn will cross-pollinate. Make corn mounds thirty to thirty-six inches apart. Use six seeds to a hill. Plant the seeds seven to eight inches apart, one inch deep. Cover tightly with one-half inch of soil. Water right after plant-

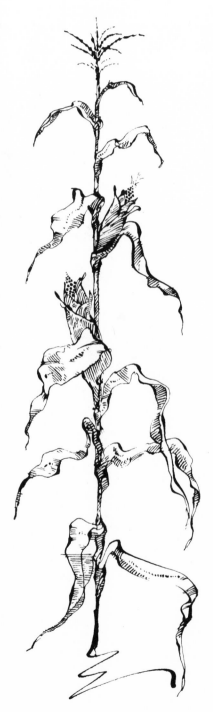

45

ing. After the corn germinates, thin to three plants per mound. Corn is ready when silk is brown and should be picked when it can be cooked immediately.

Cucumbers. Melons and squash are of the same family as cucumbers. Plant cucumbers in mounds after composting or fertilizing the soil. Put six seeds in a mound in one-inch holes, then cover tightly with one-half inch of soil. When they are three inches high, thin to three plants per mound. Harvest cucumbers when they are under six inches long because the seeds often toughen as they grow longer. Pick cucumbers often to encourage a large yield.

Eggplant. Eggplants require consistently warm weather, and a ten- to twelve-week growing period, so in cooler areas they should be planted indoors first. Plant in furrows one inch deep and cover tightly with one-half inch of soil. Thin or transplant eighteen to twenty inches apart when plants are three inches high. Fruit should be four to five inches in diameter and purple black at the time of harvest, but if the weather is unusually cool, pick them and let them ripen in a cool, dark place.

Garlic. Plant each garlic clove (use the market variety) in a one-inch-deep hole, tip up, with cloves six inches apart. Cover tightly with one-half inch of soil. Harvest when stalks wither and fall over. Lay bulbs on ground or on a platform in the sun for a week or ten days to dry or until bulb is firm and outer cover is paper thin. Braid or store in a cool, dry place.

Parsnips. Be sure soil is rich down to ten or twelve inches and plant as soon as the ground can be worked. Sow seeds one-half inch deep and cover tightly with one-half inch of soil. Thin to three inches apart when they are three inches high. Pick them as you want to cook them. They can be covered with mulch or newspapers and harvested again in the spring when the ground thaws.

46

Peas. There are both climbing peas and dwarf, or bush, peas. The latter are less work, of course, because there is no climbing apparatus necessary. Plant in four-inch-deep trenches three inches apart. Cover with one inch of soil and fill in trench as seedlings develop. Except for snow peas and the new sugar snap peas (with edible pea pods), shelled peas should be picked before the pod is too plump. They are best when they are cooked immediately after picking.

Peppers. There are many types of sweet and hot peppers in North America, but the large bell pepper is the one most commonly grown in the home garden; it is also the mildest. As the bell pepper ripens, it turns red (although in some areas they often do not get ripe enough to turn red), and as it gets redder the flavor becomes sweeter. Start peppers indoors, or wait to plant or transplant until the outdoor temperatures are consistently mild. When the plants reach three inches in height, thin to eighteen inches apart and fertilize when fruit begins to appear. Frost will kill pepper plants, so try to harvest them before the weather turns cool.

Potatoes. Potatoes like sandy soil and can be planted early. Plant in four- to six-inch trenches about eighteen inches apart. Cover with three inches of soil, and when the seedlings are six inches high, hill the earth around them to three or four inches. Harvest when the vines start to wither. Lay them out in the garden for a day, then store in a dark place.

Radishes. It seems that radishes are always the first crop of the season, and they are a sure bet for the beginning gardener. Plant the seeds shallow in fine soil. Thin when seedlings appear and harvest when they begin to show. (Radishes get woody when they are left in the ground after they are ready.)

Rutabagas. Rutabagas are a good root crop for a small garden because they can be planted early and they grow quickly, making room for another crop. Sow in furrows one inch deep and cover tightly with one-half inch of soil. Thin seedlings three to six inches apart when they are about three inches high. Harvest time depends on the variety, so consult the package. Rutabagas can be stored in damp sand in a cool, dry place.

Spinach. Spinach is sometimes temperamental, but the hardier New Zealand spinach usually responds to every gardener. (The latter variety is slower to germinate, so soak the seeds overnight before planting.) Plant regular spinach early in the spring and stagger the crop with a row of New Zealand spinach. Sow six seeds to one foot in furrows and cover tightly with fine soil. Thin seedlings to four inches or more apart when they are three inches high. Cut regular spinach from the root; cut New Zealand spinach from its vines.

Squash. Summer squash is the gardener's dream (or the neighbors' nightmare if the crop is too large for one family). If all else fails to blight and bugs, squash will prevail. Plant summer squash in one-inch-deep furrows, two seeds to every foot. Cover tightly and thin the weakest of the two seedlings when they are three inches high. Plant three or four winter squash seeds in hills four to five feet apart. Compost around winter squash vines. Pick summer squash when they are at least five inches long (or two to three inches across for round squash); the skin should be tender. Larger zucchini can be picked and stored in a cool place. Pick winter squash when the stem withers.

Tomatoes. Tomatoes are another dream crop for home gardeners. Seeds can be started inside and transplanted when the ground is warm, or small plants can be purchased. Seeds sown outside will take two to three months to produce. Sow a seed every inch in a furrow and cover tightly with fine soil. When seedlings reach four inches in height, thin to or transplant two feet apart. Compost around plant halfway through the growing season and mulch around the base of the plant to hold in moisture. Remove suckers at the bottom of the plant and between the main stalks and the branches. There are various ways to stake tomatoes. The easiest is with one substantial stake driven into the ground next to the plant so the branches can be tied to it as they grow. Also you can make Xs or tepees of thinner stakes, or circle each plant with chicken wire. Pick fruit as it matures, and gather every tomato before a frost (you can always make green tomato recipes).

Turnips. Start your turnip crop early, then another can be matured before the season ends. Plant in furrows one inch deep and cover tightly with one-half inch of soil. Thin when plants are three inches high to three to six inches apart. The early crop can be pulled in three to four weeks, but the greens can be used earlier. Harvest and store turnips as you would other root vegetables.

PLANTING, HARVESTING, AND DRYING HERBS

Since most of the herbs we use in cooking are from the Mediterranean countries, we should try to simulate the soil conditions there — poor earth, good drainage, hot sun. If you have a reliable nursery, it's easier to start your herb garden with small plants or seedlings, especially if you live in an area with a long cold season. If you want to start from seeds, it's wise to start your plants indoors, especially in cold weather. (See general information about starting seedlings indoors, p. 40.)

When harvesting your herbs each season, remember that the leaves can be picked anytime after the plant has established itself. Harvest for *drying* just as the flowers begin to bloom. Cut perennial herbs back to one-third of their size, or, if you have room, just let them grow into bushes. Annual herbs should be pulled out by the roots to make room for more seeds or plants in the next season. To dry herbs, shake off the dirt and tie the sprigs in small bunches. Hang them by the stems (upside down) in a warm, dry, well-ventilated area, out of direct sun. In a week or so crumble them between your fingers and store in covered jars in a dark place.

Besides raising herbs for your own kitchen, think of them as potential gifts — in decorative jars, sachets, or wreaths for the kitchen. If you get into the habit of raising some of your own herbs, you will discover how your cooking improves with the fresh sprigs or leaves, and how much more flavorful are home-dried herbs.

Basil (known also as *Sweet Basil*). An annual that likes more water than most herbs. Pinch back flowers as they appear to promote bushiness — likes sun or filtered sun.

Chives. A perennial that prefers a rich, moist soil and some fertilizer after cutting. Snip off top stems as needed.

Dill. An annual that likes full sun. Both leaves and seeds are usable. Pick leaves as flowers appear, and harvest seeds just as they start to drop.

Mint. A perennial that prefers filtered sun and some shade. Use a richer soil for mint. Water frequently.

Oregano. A perennial that likes full sun and lots of water with good drainage. Pinch back flowers to encourage bushiness.

Parsley. A biennial that likes filtered sun or shade, and water. Parsley grows well if it doesn't get too hot. Pick it before flowers appear and the leaves turn bitter.

Rosemary. A perennial that likes sun and good drainage. Rosemary grows forever and can be picked year round. It produces a lovely lavender flower.

Sage. A perennial that likes full sun and not much water. It grows big and bushy like rosemary and oregano, but should be cut back after flowers appear. Fertilize it as a young plant.

Tarragon. A perennial that prefers filtered sun, richer soil, and good drainage.

Thyme. A perennial that likes full sun and good drainage, spreads rapidly if not over-watered.

The Complete Book of Edible Landscaping. Rosalind Creasy. Sierra Club Books.

The Encyclopedia of Organic Gardening. Rodale Press.

Grow It and Cook It. Jacqueline Heriteau. Ballantine Books.

Hunger Signs in Crops. Howard B. Sprague, ed. David McKay Co.

Small-Space Gardens. Sunset Books.

Suggested Reading

The Well-Stocked Kitchen

PRESERVING VEGETABLES AND FRUITS

Chapter Three

The Well-Stocked Kitchen

Certainly the popularity of home gardening has re-kindled interest in canning and freezing vegetables and fruits. Even if you don't have a garden that produces an excess, home preserving is well worth the effort when you happen across a good buy on produce, or if a friend drops off a lug of fresh fruits or vegetables that are in season. In many urban areas, city dwellers are able to find good, fresh produce if they take a Sunday drive out-side the city limits. Not only has small-plot gardening been revived in this last decade, but many back-to-the-landers supplement their income by selling part of their crops. You don't have to preserve an entire winter's worth of vegetables and fruits to take advantage of the abun-dance and economy of seasonal foods; you could put enough by to have a few gifts to take to dinner parties or for holiday exchanges.

Before you get into any home canning, I would like to emphasize that the recommended canning procedure for *low-acid* vegetables and fruits is pressure canning. The early American canning method (before pressure canners were invented) was by a boiling water bath, and my mother always canned that way when I was young. It was, in fact, the way I learned to can. My father, too, tells the story of how, on the desolate plains of western North Dakota, his mother used their copper washtub as her canning kettle. And, he says, "She canned everything we ate in a water bath." Well, over the years home canning has become less common, especially with the advent of commercially canned foods and frozen foods. As a custom dies out, so do cautions, and in this case the major safeguard for water-bath canned foods in the past was that everyone recooked their canned foods; and cooking canned food for a certain amount of time will prevent botulism poisoning. (Clostridium botulism is caused by bacteria that grow in an airless container, such as a canning jar, when a nonacid food has not been properly prepared or processed long enough.) So while the nutritional trend has been not to overcook vegetables, we have also eliminated the necessary precaution for foods canned in water baths. Therefore, any person who is new to canning is wise to invest in a pressure canner, which assures the processing time by a gauge, thus avoiding any errors in judgment.

After canning, if you discover any leaking jars or jars that spurt when opened, you should discard the contents. Even though acid fruits are not subject to botulism, you should discard the contents of jars that contain moldy fruit. And it is still recommended that all home-canned nonacid vegetables (even those pressure canned) be boiled at least ten minutes before they are eaten.

Porcelain-lined screw cap   Metal screw cap   Self-sealing cap   Clamp-type lid

There are four types of jar lids used for canning. The clamp type is rare today unless you have a grandmother who has a stash. It is most commonly seen in specialty shops where it is sold dearly as a decorator item. To use the porcelain-lined screw cap and the metal screw cap lids, screw the lids on tightly, then give a quarter turn back to allow steam to escape during processing. After processing, screw the bands on tightly. The newer, self-sealing cap is screwed on tightly *before* processing. Place jars in canning pan and pour boiling water over the lids before processing. The clamp-tite cap, a glass-top variety, should be sealed partially before processing by clicking the longer wire over the top. The shorter wire is clicked down into place after processing.

PACKING

Two methods used to pack food for processing are "cold pack" and "hot pack."

Cold Pack. Prepare fruit according to Preparation Guide for Canning Fruits on page 61. Without crushing the fruit pack it tightly into jars. Pour boiling syrup or water over the fruit to within one-half inch of the top of the jar. Always cold-pack soft fruit because any precooking makes it too mushy. Process.

Hot Pack. Prepare and cook fruit or vegetables according to the guides on pages 60 and 61. Pack into jars, then cover with cooking liquid. The advantage of this method is that you don't waste jar space since the food is already cooked and won't shrink during processing.

PROCESSING

Water Bath. Make sure your canning pot is thoroughly clean. Screw or clamp on the lids (see Types of Containers above) after jars have been filled and place the jars on a rack in a large pot containing hot, not boiling, water. The water should come to the necks of the jars, and the jars should not touch each other (touching may cause them to break). Bring the water to a boil, and gauge the cooking time from the moment boiling begins. Keep at a gentle boil, adding more water if necessary. Keep the pot lid tightly closed during processing because the heat sterilizes and seals the jar lids. If you are using a standard canning pan for processing fruit, place additional filled jars in the pan as soon as the previous batch has finished so you have a continuous flow.

Pressure canning. Thoroughly clean pressure cooker. If you have a dial gauge, be sure to have it checked before you begin canning and several times during the season if you do a lot of canning. (Ask your dealer where to have the gauge checked.) Place jars in the cooker, which should contain about three inches of water. Leave space between each jar so the steam can circulate freely. Attach cover and turn on heat. Exhaust all air within the cooker by letting a steady flow of steam escape for ten minutes before closing the petcock. Start counting processing time when the gauge reaches the specified pressure. You *must* keep pressure constant by adjusting heat; otherwise the liquid will be drawn from the jars. Turn off heat when time is up. Do not open cooker until pressure gauge registers 0. Then open the petcock slowly to allow remaining steam to escape. Remove cover.

SIMPLE CANNING STEPS FOR FRUITS AND VEGETABLES

1. Check all jars for nicks and cracks. Use new rubber rings for the porcelain-lined screw cap, the metal screw cap, and the clamp-tite lid, and new caps for the self-sealing lids (see page 56).

2. Wash and scald jars and lids.

3. Select and wash firm, ripe produce. Prepare according to the guides on pages 60 and 61.

4. Pack fruit or vegetables into jars, leaving proper head space — one inch for starchy foods (corn, peas, beans) and one-half inch for fruits and other vegetables.

5. Add liquid. Release air bubbles by running a knife around the inside of the jars.

6. Wipe the necks of the jars completely clean and put on scalded lids. Remember to give a quarter turn back with rubber-ring jars (or leave unclamped) and to pour boiling water over self-sealing lids.

7. Process jars in water bath or pressure cooker. Follow recipes and instructions carefully.

8. Remove jars after the required amount of time and set them on wood, Formica, or folded towels.

9. Immediately tighten or clamp rubber-ring jars and let all jars cool for twelve hours.

10. After twelve hours, you can remove metal screw bands (if you wish to use them on other jars) from the self-sealing type of jars. All metal lids seal soon after the processing, and you can usually hear a click as the lid is drawn down, but it's wise to press the cap lightly to aid this process. If the lid stays down, the seal is good. There is a distinct difference between the sound of a sealed lid and an unsealed lid. The latter sounds hollow; the sealed lid rings if you tap it with a spoon. Reprocess or refrigerate (and use soon after) jars that do not seal.

CANNING HINTS

1. Pierce unpeeled fruit to prevent skin from bursting.

2. Remove fruit or tomato skin by dropping fruit into boiling water for a minute or so until the skin comes off easily.

3. If possible, pack halved fruit center-side down to prevent syrup from filling center cavity and to insure tighter packing.

4. Do not put freshly canned jars that are still hot in a draft or on cold metal counters; they might crack.

5. For variation add sliced lemon to jars of pears, cinnamon sticks to apricots or peaches.

6. Do not fill jars too full, or liquid will be forced out during the processing.

7. For flavor add two or three pits to each jar when canning apricots.

FREEZING FRUITS AND VEGETABLES

Freezing fruits and vegetables is easy if you follow these simple steps:

1. Select firm, fresh, ripe produce. Cut away any bad spots.

2. Try to do the preparation in the early morning or in the cool evening immediately after the produce has been picked or purchased. The heat of the day tends to wilt vegetables and fruits.

3. Fruits and vegetables should be clean and packed very tightly to prevent air pockets.

(continued on page 62)

Preparation Guide for Canning Vegetables

Vegetable	Preparation (Add one teaspoon salt to each quart of vegetables and use cooking water to fill jar unless otherwise specified.)	Pressure Canning Minutes at 10 lbs.
Asparagus	Wash, precook 3 minutes in boiling water, tips above water, pack hot.	pts. — 25 qts. — 40
Beans green, wax	Wash, cut off ends and strings, cut in 1-inch pieces, precook 5 minutes, pack hot.	pts. — 20 qts. — 25
lima	Shell and wash lima beans, cover with water, bring to a boil, pack hot and loosely.	pts. — 25 qts. — 60
Beets	Wash, cut off leaves, retaining 1-inch stem, precook 15 minutes, slip off skins, leave whole or slice. Pack hot.	pts. — 25 qts. — 45
Broccoli	Remove outside leaves, wash, precook 3 minutes, pack hot using fresh boiling water.	pts. — 35 qts. — 40
Brussels sprouts	Wash, precook 3 minutes, pack hot using fresh boiling water.	pts. — 35 qts. — 40
Cabbage	Wash, peel off outer leaves, cut in small wedges, precook for 3 minutes, pack hot using fresh boiling water.	pts. — 35 qts. — 40
Cauliflower	Break into flowerets, precook 3 minutes, pack hot using fresh boiling water.	pts. — 30 qts. — 40
Corn	Cut kernels from cob, add one pint boiling water to each quart of corn, heat to boil, pack hot and loosely.	pts. — 85 qts. — 85
Greens (all types)	Wash, remove tough stems, steam until wilted, pack hot and cut an X through greens to remove air pockets.	pts. — 45 qts. — 70
Parsnips	Wash and pare, precook 5 minutes, cut in 1/2-inch cubes or slice thinly, pack hot.	pts. — 20 qts. — 35
Peas	Shell and wash, cover with boiling water, bring to a boil, pack hot and loosely.	pts. — 40 qts. — 40
Potatoes	Wash, peel, cut in 1-inch cubes, precook 2 minutes, pack hot. (Precook new potatoes 5 minutes.)	pts. — 40 qts. — 40
Squash (all types)	Wash, peel winter squash, precook until tender, pack hot.	pts. — 55 qts. — 90
Sweet potatoes or Yams	Wash, cook in boiling water until skins slip, peel, cut in 2-inch cubes, pack hot.	pts. — 65 qts. — 95
Tomatoes	Scald and slip skins, pack whole or cut in pieces, pack hot.	pts. — 20* qts. — 30*
Turnips	Wash and pare, precook 5 minutes, cut in 1/2-inch cubes or slice thinly, pack hot.	pts. — 20 qts. — 35

*Water-bath processing time.

Preparation Guide for Canning Fruits

Fruit can be packed in syrup, in fruit juice, or in water (for those who prefer the natural taste). When you use syrup, prepare it in advance and pour it boiling hot over the fruit. Honey is not necessarily recommended for syrup because of its prohibitive cost today.

Syrup	Honey	Sugar	Water
Thin	1/2	1	3 parts
Medium	1/2	1	2 parts

Fruit	Preparation	Water Bath Minutes for pts./qts.	Pressure Canning Minutes at 5 lbs.
Apples	Pare, core, slice, precook 5 minutes, pack hot, cover with hot syrup or water, *or*	15	10
	Bake, cover with hot syrup, *or*	15	5
	Make applesauce, pack hot.	10	5
Apricots	Wash, halve, pit. Pack uncooked and cover with hot syrup, *or*	35	10
	Heat through in medium syrup and pack hot.	20	5
Blackberries	Wash, pack, cover with hot syrup.	20	8
Blueberries, dewberries, huckleberries, loganberries, raspberries	Wash, pack, cover with hot syrup.	15	5
Cherries	Wash, stem, do not pit, pack, cover with hot syrup.	20	10
Peaches	Wash, halve, pit, pack uncooked, cover with hot syrup (or scald and slip skins first), *or*	35	10
	Wash, halve, pit, precook 5 minutes in syrup, pack hot.	20	8
Pears	Wash, halve, core. Pack uncooked, cover with boiling syrup, *or*	35	10
	Wash, halve, core, precook 5 minutes in syrup, pack hot.	20	8
Plums	Wash, do not pit or peel, prick skins, pack uncooked, cover with hot syrup, *or,*	15	5
	Wash, precook 5 minutes in syrup, pack hot.	10	5
Rhubarb	Wash, cut into pieces, precook in syrup until tender, pack hot.	10	5

4. Allow one inch of head space for expansion, using plastic freezing containers of moisture- and vaporproof, or resistant, wrappings. Follow any manufacturer's directions for wrapping and sealing.

5. Store at 0°F. or below. At that temperature you can keep fruits and vegetables for approximately twelve months. It's best to freeze small packages because they freeze more quickly.

PREPARATION GUIDE FOR FREEZING VEGETABLES

1. Use only fresh, washed vegetables.

2. Scald or blanch in boiling water to stop the fermentation action that causes color and flavor changes. You do not need a blancher; simply use a large pan of boiling water (eight times the amount of water to the amount of vegetables) and a metal colander or wire basket for holding the vegetables. Immerse vegetables in water and time the scalding carefully from the moment the water returns to a boil.

3. Immediately after scalding, plunge the vegetables into ice water, or hold under cold running water.

4. Drain and pack closely in plastic cartons or freezer bags. Leave about one inch of head space for expansion. Otherwise eliminate as much air as possible.

5. Freeze at 0°F. or below.

6. When ready to use, cook from the frozen stage as you would commercially frozen vegetables. If you wish to use frozen vegetables in salad, simply dip vegetables in boiling water until thawed.

7. Do not salt vegetables until serving.

Asparagus. Wash well and break off ends at the tender point. Scald two to three minutes, depending on the thickness of the spears. Chill for three times the scalding time.

Beans (green or wax). Select young, tender beans. Wash. Cut off stem and blossom ends. Scald French-cut beans (cut diagonally in thin slices) about one minute. Scald yellow wax beans one-half minute longer. Scald whole green beans for three minutes. Chill three times the length of scalding time.

Beets. Cut off tops, leaving a bit of the top as a finger hold. (See "Spinach and Other Greens" for instructions

62

for freezing beet tops.) Cook beets in very little water until the skins slip. Spread on a tray to cool. Peel and slice large beets; pack baby beets whole.

Broccoli. Cut stalks the length of the container. Rinse. Trim tough parts from cut-off ends and cut into uniform pieces. Scald stalks and pieces separately for three to five minutes, depending on thickness. Chill rapidly in ice water.

Brussels sprouts. Sort according to size and wash well to remove any insects. Scald from three to four minutes, depending on size. Chill in ice water three times as long as the scalding time.

Cauliflower. Trim into florets. Wash well or let stand in light salt water brine for ten minutes. Scald for three to four minutes, depending on size. Chill immediately in ice water.

Corn on the cob. Use young, juicy ears. Husk and remove all the silk. Scald by dropping a few ears into rapidly boiling water for seven to ten minutes, depending on size. Chill immediately for three times the scalding time to make sure the cob is well cooled. Do not freeze more than two ears together. To cook: drop ears into a large quantity of cold water and bring the water slowly to a boil in order to thaw out the cob without overcooking the kernels. Boil for not more than two minutes because corn overcooks easily. If you have frozen the corn in foil, brush with butter, rewrap, and roast in moderate oven for twenty to twenty-five minutes.

Corn (whole kernels). Scald the corn on the cob for two to three minutes. Chill immediately in ice water or under cold running water. Cut corn from the cob.

Peas. Use only very young peas. Shell and scald for one to two minutes. Chill immediately and dry well before freezing.

Peppers. Use sweet peppers. Remove stems and seeds. Wash. Cut into small pieces and freeze without scalding. If you wish to freeze whole stuffed peppers, scald seeded peppers for three to five minutes. Chill in ice water or under cold running water. Drain and stuff with cooked filling. Wrap. Keep frozen for not more than four months.

Spinach and Other Greens. Wash well. Scald or steam

only long enough to wilt the green. Quickly chill in ice water if scalded or in the refrigerator if steamed.

Summer squash. Select very young squash with tender skins. Wash. Trim blossom and stem ends. Cut into four-inch pieces and scald for two minutes or steam for three minutes. Chill quickly in ice water.

Tomatoes. Tomatoes lose their natural texture when frozen. I recommend canning them if you come into a good supply. Otherwise, make tomato soup and freeze it, or make relishes or tomato paste. If you do have freezer room, you can freeze whole tomatoes without peeling, slicing, or coring them. Just wash and place them uncovered in the freezer. To use, run cold water over them to slip the skins. They will be good for cooking, but too mushy for salads.

PREPARATION GUIDE FOR FREEZING FRUITS

1. For fruit that discolors easily, prepare no more than five cups at a time.

2. A sharp freeze (below 0°F.) is best for most fruit, providing the fruit is reasonably cool to begin with.

3. When ready to use, thaw fruit slowly, starting in the refrigerator.

Apples. Peel (if not organically grown), core, and slice. Apples will turn dark if they are the least bit green; therefore, sprinkle with lemon sugar or powdered ascorbic or citric acid (available from druggists). Pack tightly.

Apricots. Wash, halve, and pit apricots. To preserve color, you may use a light syrup made of lemon juice and sugar, or honey, and water, or sprinkle with lemon juice.

Berries. Berries should be firm, well cleaned, and free of stems and leaves. Strawberries should be sugared, but sweetening is not necessary for other berries. Crumple wax paper to put in the top of freezer containers in order to exclude as much air as possible.

Oranges. Peel, section or slice, and sugar lightly.

Peaches and Pears. Blanch to remove skin. Pit or core and prepare the same as apricots.

Plums. Wash. Whole plums do not need sugar for freezing, but it is wise to steam them slightly to keep their skins from getting tough.

64

Following are the definitions of the various accompaniments to food: jam, an unstrained fruit spread; jelly, a strained fruit spread; marmalade, a jamlike spread made from citrus fruits, juice, and the rind; fruit butter, a spread that is cooked smooth to spread easily; conserve, a sweet jamlike relish made from fruits with nuts and raisins; relish, a tart mixture made from vegetables; chutney, a hot relish of East Indian origin made from fruits, vegetables, and spices; and preserve, whole fruit cooked with sugar where the fruit remains intact and the jelly is clear and thick.

All jars of spreads and relishes can be sealed by using self-sealing lids and a short, hot-water bath (see page 57), or by sealing with paraffin. (Jar manufacturers include instructions for using self-sealing lids.) If you wish to seal jars with paraffin, heat the paraffin in a double boiler. If the paraffin is too hot, it will pull away from the edge of the jar as it cools, making an imperfect seal. Pour the melted paraffin one-quarter-inch thick over the surface of the jam and let it set for a day. The next day pour a slightly thinner layer over the first; this procedure insures a proper seal. Jams and jellies that have cooked a long time should be allowed to cool slightly before the paraffin is added; but those made with pectin, as well as conserves and relishes, should not remain long without sealing as they can mold rapidly.

When using fruits that are high in natural pectin, such as cranberries, apples, plums, and quinces, the slow-cooking oven method for making jam works best. Fruits that are low in pectin (pears, peaches, apricots, grapes, cherries, figs, pineapples, and berries — except gooseberries and cranberries) should be combined with the high-pectin fruits or prepared by using commercial or homemade pectin. If you wish to make your own pectin from apples, you can use the recipe included in this chapter. To insure that the jam will set, put it in a ten- to fifteen-minute hot-water bath. The instructions that follow are for making jam and jelly without pectin. If you decide to use pectin, follow the directions on the pectin package.

Wash fruit, remove cores or pits, mash, and add an equal amount of sugar. Spread mixture in a shallow baking pan and put it in a slow oven (250°) for five to six hours, or until it thickens. Stir occasionally. Pour into sterilized jars with self-sealing lids, or seal with paraffin.

Honey may be used instead of sugar, but the jam will not thicken very much with low-pectin fruits unless you use extra pectin. Use only two-thirds the amount of honey to the amount of sugar called for in the recipe. A little lemon juice enhances the flavor of jams, and the acid assists in the jelling.

MAKING JAM WITHOUT PECTIN

Place washed, prepared fruit in a stainless steel or enamel pan. (Small amounts of jam should be made at a time for the best results.) Add a little water, not more than one-half cup, if fruit is dry. Simmer fruit until it begins to soften, then add sugar (see following chart for amount). Bring the mixture to a boil and stir for a few seconds before reducing heat. Cook and simmer fruit, stirring occasionally, until it is thickened (about thirty to thirty-five minutes). Do not let it burn. Pour thickened jam into sterilized jars. Seal with paraffin or use self-sealing lids. (Screw metal rings tight, pour boiling water over lids and press lids down with your finger.)

MAKING JELLY WITHOUT PECTIN

Wash fruit very well and let it drain. Peel fruit if appropriate and remove cores or pits. Cut up into small pieces. Juicy fruits need very little additional water, but fruits such as apples and pears require slightly more (one-half to three-quarters cup to two quarts fruit), but not so much that the fruit swims in water. Place in heavy-bottomed pot. Start the cooking process over very low heat, increase heat as the juice is drawn out of the fruit, and keep the heat at medium for twenty to thirty minutes. The time varies, depending on the fruit.

Fold together three thicknesses of cheesecloth and lay them in a strainer. Pour in the fruit to slowly strain out the juice, exerting a little pressure — not too much or the jelly will not be clear. The strained juice can be made into jelly immediately or frozen for later use. You can even save a little juice to combine with the remaining fruit to make jam.

To make a firm jelly from the strained juice, return the juice to a large pan (enamel or stainless steel) and simmer for several minutes. Skim off any froth and add sugar according to the recipe you are using (or see the following chart). Simmer. When the sugar has dissolved, bring to a boil and stir until the jellying point is reached. Test for the jellying point by cooling a little of the mixture on a spoon. It should fall in one heavy drop if it is ready to be put into jars. Pour into sterilized jars with self-sealing lids, or seal with paraffin.

Fruit	Juice	Sugar
Apple	1 cup	3/4 cup
Berry	1 cup	3/4 to 1 cup
Crab apple	1 cup	3/4 cup
Cranberry	1 cup	3/4 cup
Currant	1 cup	3/4 to 1 cup
Grape	1 cup	3/4 to 1 cup

HOMEMADE PECTIN

Fully ripened apples make a clear pectin, but the pectin made from early, small green apples thickens best. The approximate yield is one quart of pectin from one pound of apples.

Wash and core apples. Cut in thin slices. Add one pint of water per pound of apples and boil slowly in a covered pot for fifteen minutes.

Strain the free-flowing juice through light muslin or cheesecloth. Return the pulp to the pot, adding an equal amount of water. Cook slowly for another fifteen minutes. Strain the juice through the cloth again, this time squeezing the pulp dry.

Combine the two strained juices and use immediately, or bring to a full boil, pour into sterilized jars, and seal with paraffin, like jam, for later use. Use one cup of this pectin to six cups of prepared fruit in your jam or jelly recipes.

Uncooked Grape Jelly

1 quart grapes
14 cups water
sugar

Put grapes and water in saucepan. Simmer until fruit is soft. Lay a thin cloth in a colander that is placed over a pan; pour in softened fruit and mash to extract juice. Measure in sugar, 1/2 cup sugar to 1 cup juice. Beat 10 minutes with a spoon to dissolve sugar, then pour into sterilized jars. Cover and store in the refrigerator. Uncooked grape jelly jells in 3 to 4 days and makes 8 to 10 pints.

Fresh Berry Jam

3-1/2 to 4 cups fresh raspberries or strawberries
honey to taste
1 package pectin

Mash berries, then place them in a blender with honey. Add pectin and blend briskly for about 2 minutes. Pour into sterilized jars and store in the refrigerator.

Orange Marmalade

2 large oranges
2 large lemons
2-1/2 quarts water
8 cups sugar

Scrub oranges and lemons well, chop into pieces, and remove all seeds. Cover with water and let soak for 24 to 28 hours. Remove fruit and cut into very small pieces, shredding the rind. Return fruit and rind to soaking water and bring to a boil. Keep at a slow boil for an hour, then add sugar. Continue to boil until marmalade tests with a spoon (see "Making Jelly Without Pectin," p. 66). Pour into sterilized jars with self-sealing lids, or seal with paraffin. Makes 6 to 8 pints.

Fruit Syrup

1. Wash fruit well. Peel if the fruit has thick or toughened skins, core or pit, and cut into pieces.
2. Put a small amount in the blender and puree. Repeat until all fruit is used.
3. Force pureed fruit through a wire strainer.
4. To every 4 cups of strained fruit puree add:
1 cup water

3 tablespoons lemon juice
3 cups sugar, or 1-1/2 to 2 cups honey (decrease
    amount if a less-sweet syrup is desired)
    5. Bring all ingredients to a boil and cook for 2
minutes, stirring constantly.
    6. Remove from heat, skim off the foam, pour
into sterilized jars, and seal.

Apple Butter

    1. Wash, core, and cut apples into small pieces.
    2. Put into a pot with a little water (very little,
only enough to prevent burning) and cook over
low heat until apples are softened.
    3. Put through a sieve or wire strainer.
    4. To each 4 cups of apple pulp add 2 cups
sugar.
    5. Cook slowly over low heat until thick
(several hours), either on top of the stove or in
a shallow pan in a 250° oven.
    6. When thickened, add 1 teaspoon cinnamon
and 1/2 teaspoon each allspice and cloves to each
4 cups of apple butter. Pour into sterilized jars
and seal.

Rhubarb Conserve

4 cups diced rhubarb
1 cup raisins
1 tablespoon grated orange rind
1/4 cup orange juice
3 cups sugar
1/2 cup nuts
To rhubarb add all ingredients except nuts.
Cook, stirring occasionally, until juice is thick
and clear. Add nuts, pour mixture into hot,
sterilized jars, and seal immediately. Makes
about 4 pints.

Tomato Relish

2 quarts ripe tomatoes
1 cup chopped celery
1 cup chopped white onions
2 cups diced tart apples
2 red peppers, seeded and chopped
2 green peppers, seeded and chopped
1-1/2 cups vinegar
1-3/4 cups sugar
1 tablespoon salt
1 tablespoon broken cinnamon sticks

1/2 tablespoon whole cloves
2 tablespoons white mustard seeds
Scald, peel, and chop tomatoes. Add all other
ingredients. Boil, stirring occasionally, until
mixture is thickened. Pour into sterilized jars
and seal. Makes 4 to 5 pints.

English Chutney

1 dozen ripe tomatoes
1 pound apples, cored
3/4 pound raisins
2 sweet red peppers, seeded
6 small onions
1/4 cup mint leaves
1/4 cup white mustard seeds
1-1/2 tablespoons salt
2 cups sugar
1 quart vinegar
Chop tomatoes. Put other vegetables and mint
leaves through a food chopper or meat grinder.
Combine all ingredients in a large pot and bring
to a boil. Cook slowly until mixture becomes
thick and clear. Pour into sterilized jars and
seal. Makes about 2-1/2 quarts.

Tomato Paste

4 quarts tomatoes
1 to 4 cloves of garlic
1 teaspoon cayenne pepper
2 sweet red peppers, seeded
salt to taste
2 tablespoons oil (optional)
Wash ripe tomatoes and slice without peeling.
Add all other ingredients except oil and cook
until soft. Put through a coarse sieve. Return to
pot and simmer the pulp, stirring frequently,
until it is the consistency of thick catsup. Place in
the top of a double boiler and continue to cook
over hot water until mixture becomes the thickness of paste. Add oil if desired and pack into
sterilized jars (half-pint jars are best) and seal.
Makes 4 to 5 pints.

Zucchini Pickles

2 quarts thinly sliced, unpeeled, small zucchini
2 medium onions, peeled and thinly sliced
1/4 cup salt
water

2 cups vinegar
1 cup sugar
1 teaspoon celery seeds
2 teaspoons mustard seeds
1 teaspoon tumeric
1/2 teaspoon dry mustard

These look and taste like fine bread-and-butter pickles. Combine zucchini and onions, sprinkle with salt, and cover with cold water. Let stand 2 hours, drain, rinse with fresh water, then drain again. Combine remaining ingredients in a large pot and bring to boiling. Cook 2 minutes. Add vegetables, remove from heat, and let stand 2 hours. Bring again to boiling and cook 5 minutes. Pack into sterilized jars and seal. Makes 4 to 5 pints.

Fresh Tomato Salsa

2 small tomatoes, unpeeled
1/2 medium onion, chopped
1 to 2 fresh chiles serranos or 1 fresh jalapeno chile
1/4 cup chopped cilantro
2 tablespoons cold water
salt to taste

Chop tomatoes and mix with chopped onions and chiles that have not been seeded. Add cilantro, water, and salt to taste. Makes about 1-1/2 to 1-3/4 cups.

Suggested Reading

Canning, Freezing, & Drying. Sunset Books.
Home Food Systems. Roger B. Yepson, ed. Rodale Press.
Putting Foods By. Ruth Hertzberg, Beatrice Vaughan, and Janet Greene. Bantam Books and Stephen Greene Press.

CHAPTER FOUR
The Economical Kitchen
FOOD SHOPPING AND STORAGE

Chapter Four

The Economical Kitchen

Nearly every household — rural, urban, or suburban — has to rely on some commercial sources for food staples. For most of us this means a weekly trip (at least) to the supermarket. Don't fret if you are in this category, for it's possible to obtain all the ingredients for a good diet in a modern supermarket, providing your market has a good selection of the basic ingredients of the four food groups. There are, however, other food sources that you might want to look into, depending on where you live.

For example, mail-order foods are becoming popular these days, especially for obtaining exotic or ethnic ingredients. However, this is not necessarily an area of economy and probably should be considered only when such ingredients that you feel are essential to a favorite family menu are not available locally. More often, you might wish to turn to mail-order buying when you want to obtain whole grains and flours directly from a mill when you cannot find them in your local markets. (A list of some of these sources is included at the end of this chapter.)

As I have already mentioned, buying from truck farmers and at small stands outside the city is a good way to obtain fresh eggs, chickens, rabbits, and produce. Country shopping makes a nice family outing and is a great way of getting the freshest food. Too, many people in my area buy meat in large sections from local meat lockers. The meat is then cup up, ground, and wrapped for freezing. It's stored in commercial lockers, which they rent, or in their home freezers. This is an especially economical practice for people who eat a lot of meat and a good way to obtain top-quality food.

Still, for most of us the common food source is a local supermarket, where, if you are observant, you can often buy economically in case lots or on the days when there are specials. Here are some general supermarket tips that may be helpful in reorganizing your "whole kitchen." If your children are helping with the food shopping, it's a good idea to post the tips on your kitchen bulletin board.

1. Don't overbuy foods that can get stale or rancid without refrigeration. On the other hand, large packages of pasta, whole grains and cereals, apples, oranges, onions, potatoes — or any food that can be stored without refrigeration — are usually good buys. If you have sufficient freezer space, the larger packages of frozen vegetables are also economical, but avoid those that are "block frozen," because the "block" indicates that the vegetables have thawed in transit and have then been refrozen. Produce that has been continually frozen is loose in the package.

2. Don't be taken in by food labels bearing "new," "improved," "natural," or "organically grown," or any testimony to better nutritional value. These claims are often not valid. Read the list of ingredients on the can, box, or package and choose foods that have the least chemicals and unfamiliar-sounding ingredients. Generally, the simpler and more recognizable the list of ingredients, the more healthful and natural the food. As a rule, ingredients are listed according to their volume in the particular product. You will be amazed how many products list sugar and water in the top three ingredients.

3. Pay attention to the weight/price ratio. There are many packaged rice and pasta dishes that cost quite a bit more than plain rice and pasta because they have a few added herbs and spices or an attractive picture on the box. You can duplicate these simple preparations at home at far less expense. (Who says the food industry can cook better than you?)

4. It's difficult to determine freshness in food products because coding practices vary from company to company. Dairy products are usually most consistent and are stamped with a flat shelf (or refrigeration) life date. Generally, there is a 0, then the number of the month, 07, followed by the day of the month, 07-25. Sometimes the

76

year is included, especially if it is near the end of the calendar year. This example means the product is guaranteed until July 25, although it may remain fresh considerably longer. It also means it should be removed from the market shelf after that date. The codes are on the top, sides, or bottom of the product. (In my area they are on the bottom.) Some food items have two dates, one indicating when the food was packaged, the other the day by which it should be sold. However, these dates are sometimes reversed, so it looks as if that particular item should have been sold two months ago. Always ask if you are confused.

Other codes are more elaborate. The letters of the alphabet might replace the number of the month (April is D, for example). Or the days of the year will be numbered (001 to 365, for example). Obviously, coding practices are still not in the best interests of the consumer or they would be uniform. Furthermore, there are many items that are still not visibly coded. (Do not be confused by the thick and thin black lines on a package; these are the manufacturer's identification and suggested prices; they are decoded by the retailer with electronic equipment.)

5. Besides checking the coding on food, it's important to develop a good idea of freshness and to buy only foods you can store properly and use during the time of their optimum quality. Choose fresh produce that is clean and free from defects, bruises, and blemishes. Buy meats that are graded and have been inspected by the USDA. (This inspection assures that the meat came from healthy animals and was processed under sanitary conditions.) Also, check the thermometer in the meat cases to see that the meats are held at a temperature of 40° F., or below, while on display. Buy clean eggs with no cracks, and packages and cans that are not broken, dented, rusted, or bulging.

6. Weekly specials are good only if they are foods with nutritional value and relate to your particular diet and menu plan. Unfortunately, many specials are empty-calorie foods that beguile the consumer just because they are displayed as a bargain. If you shop according to the food groups and try to plan a balanced weekly menu, it's

easier to be a more trap-resistant supermarketer.

7. It's also wise to ask the markets about their house brands. Often a chain market will carry its own brand name on items throughout the store, each costing a few cents less than the leading brand. This can add up to a big savings over a period of time, and you may even find that these house products are packaged and canned by the leading brand. (This is a common practice in all American retailing and not just confined to food products.) More recently, some markets have started carrying foods with very plain packaging, which are even more economical.

FOOD STORAGE

In spite of modern refrigeration and kitchen design, many people still lose a lot of food to improper storage. Possibly this is because they don't know where to store various foods and how long they can sit before they lose their quality and nutritive value.

Some kinds of spoilage are harmful to your health; others are not. Unfortunately, it is not always possible to distinguish (as in the case of botulism poisoning when spoilage is not evident at all). For example, unpalatable, but nonhazardous, spoilage is indicated by a rancid odor caused by oxidation slime on meat. Another example of nonhazardous spoilage is the fermentation of fruit juices due to yeast growth. On the other hand, some unpleasant odors or a sharp, sour taste in bland foods may indicate dangerous spoilage. Different foods need different temperatures and humidity to insure quality in storage; but, in general, lower temperatures are usually better because they retard the growth of spoilage organisms.

Naturally, fresh foods keep best in the refrigerator, but as I mentioned in the section on garden harvesting, some root vegetables keep adequately in damp sand in root-cellar-like conditions. Most small gardeners do not have enough of a harvest to need storage for any length of time, but if you are interested in learning more about root cellars and storage, consult the suggested reading list at the end of this chapter. My mother tells wonderful stories of the root cellar her family had when she was a child where they stored everything, including meat that was packed in tallow. And they kept dairy products in the water tank by the barn. But, of course, that was long before refrigerators, or even iceboxes.

If you don't have refrigerator space, find the coolest, darkest place to put your root vegetables, or buy only small quantities at a time. Green leafy vegetables stay crisp and high in nutrients when they are stored in cold, moist areas. However, too much moisture around certain fruits encourages the growth of mold. Use plastic bags or containers to store foods that should be kept moist, and don't wash berries or cherries until you are ready to use them. Any food that dries with exposure to air should be kept covered. Check the temperature in your refrigerator occasionally to make sure it stays constant.

Following is a general guide for food that is to be stored. These limits are general and conservative, and foods can often be kept longer if the storage is proper and temperature constant. Primarily, storage limits are to preserve nutrients. Anything that is "soupable" can be put into a pot and boiled twenty minutes to kill any bacterial contamination, but remember that any food that has been sitting on the stove for over two hours should be reheated to above 165°. Be especially careful with meat, poultry, fish, stuffings, and dairy products.

Cupboard Storage

Food Item	Storage Time
Baking powder and soda	15 months in closed containers
Bouillon, powder and cubes	1 year (best to refrigerate)
Breads	3 to 5 days
Bread crumbs (stale)	6 months
Cakes	2 to 3 days, covered
Canned foods	1 year, unopened
Cereals	
prepared, dry	1 month
to cook	6 months
Coffee	
ground	1 year (after opening refrigerate and keep 3 weeks)
instant	6 months (but keep only 2 weeks after opening)
beans	1 month (do not refrigerate)

Cookies, crackers	2 weeks in unopened or tight container
Flours	
unbleached	8 months in unopened or tight container
whole grain	6 months (refrigerate)
Fruit, dried	6 months in tight container
Herbs and spices	
whole	1 year
ground	6 months (refrigerate red spices)
Honey, molasses	1 year, tightly covered
Jams, syrups	6 months, tightly covered
Milk, dry	6 months
Oils, salad	3 months (refrigerate after opening and keep 4 months)
Pasta	1 year
Parmesan (or Romano) cheese, grated	1 month (refrigerate to keep longer)
Peanut butter	
hydrogenated	6 months unopened (keeps 2 months after opening)
nonhydrogenated	6 months unopened (refrigerate after opening, keeps 3 months)
Pastries	2 to 3 days (refrigerate cream or custard items)
Rice	
brown	1 year
white	2 years
Sugar	
brown	4 months
white	2 years
Tea, bags and loose	6 months

Refrigerator Storage

The temperature in a refrigerator should be between 35° F. and 40° F. If it rises above 40°, spoilage can occur rapidly. If it drops, produce will begin to bruise. Keep foods wrapped or covered because odors transfer from food to food in the refrigerator.

Dairy Products	Storage Time
Butter	2 weeks
Buttermilk, yogurt, sour cream	2 weeks

Cheese
cottage, ricotta	1 week
cream, spreads	2 weeks
cuts	6 weeks

Cream	1 week (if it sours, use in baked goods)

Eggs
in shell	3 weeks
whites and yolks	5 days

Milk
evaporated, opened can	1 week
whole, skim, nonfat	1 week

Meat, Poultry, and Fish	*Storage Time*
Beef, lamb, pork, veal chops, steaks, roasts, ground	
meat, stew meat	5 days
variety meats	2 days
Bacon, sandwich meats	1 week
Dry sausage	3 weeks
Ham	
unopened can	6 months
whole	1 week
pieces, slices	3 days
Poultry, fresh or thawed frozen	2 days
Fish	1 day (prepare on day of purchase, or next at latest)

Fresh Vegetables	*Storage Time*
Asparagus	4 days
Broccoli, brussels sprouts, green onions, summer squash	5 days
Cabbage, cauliflower, celery, cucumbers, eggplant, green beans, peppers, tomatoes	1 week
Corn	3 days in husk
Leafy greens	6 days (do not wash)
Lima beans, peas	5 days
Root vegetables — beets, carrots, parsnips, radishes, rutabagas, turnips	2 weeks

Fresh Fruits*	Storage Time
Apples	1 month
Apricots, avocados, bananas, grapes, melons, nectarines, peaches, plums	5 days
Berries, cherries	4 days
Citrus fruits, pineapple	2 weeks

*It is best to ripen all fruit before refrigerating.

Miscellaneous Foods	Storage Time
Cooked or canned foods (stored in refrigerator containers)	5 days
Meat chops, steaks, roasts	5 days
Ground meats, stews	3 days
Sausage, variety meats	2 days
Poultry, fish	2 days
Soups, stews, sauces, stuffings	3 days
Fruits, vegetables	3 days
Fruit juices	1 week
Cream pies or cakes	2 days
Nuts, shelled	6 months
Pickles, olives	1 month (in jars or refrigerator containers)
Potato salad, cole slaw	2 days
Wine	
table	1 week
cooking	3 months

Freezer Storage

A freezer must be kept at 0° F. when storing food more than a week or two. For any foods that you wish to store for longer than three weeks, cover with a freezer wrap or heavy foil. Foods may last longer than the time shown on this chart, but their flavors will begin to diminish. For best results do not refreeze food that has thawed, and never cook or eat any foods that have a suspicious odor or color.

Food Item	Storage Time
Breads, baked or dough	3 months (homemade dough should be baked after one month)

Butter, margarine	9 months
Cakes, cookies, cookie dough	3 months (commercial cakes last a little longer)
Cottage cheese (dry), ricotta	2 weeks (do not freeze creamy cheese as its consistency changes)
Natural cheeses	3 months
Cream	2 months (whipping cream may not whip well)
Fish	4 months (shrimp and hard-shelled crab will last a year)
Ice cream, sherbet	1 month
Cooked dishes	
meat, fish	3 months
poultry	6 months
Meat	
bacon	1 month
ground meat, stew meat	3 months
beef roasts, steaks	1 year
ham	2 months
chops	9 months
pork steaks, roasts, chops	4 months
Nuts, shelled	3 months
Pies, baked or unbaked	8 months (do not freeze home-made custard or cream pies)
Poultry	
whole, uncooked	1 year
parts, uncooked	8 months
cooked with gravy	4 months
cooked without gravy	1 month
Vegetables, fruits	
home frozen	1 year
commercially frozen	8 months

Suggested Reading *Back to the Basics: How to Learn and Enjoy Traditional American Skills.* Norman Mack, ed. Reader's Digest Association.

The Supermarket Handbook. David Goldbeck and Nikki Goldberg. Harper and Row Publishers, Inc.

Mail-Order Sources for Whole Grain Byrd Mill Co., P.O. Box 5169, Richmond, VA 23220

The Quaker Valley Mills, Quakertown, Bucks County, PA 18951

Arrowhead Mills, Inc., P.O. Box 866, Hereford, TX 79045

El Molino Mills, 3060 West Valley Boulevard, Alhambra, CA 91803

CHAPTER FIVE
The Physical Kitchen
CREATING A WORKABLE STUDIO

PROCHNOW

A look into a kitchen is always an insight into a lifestyle. Not only do our kitchens tell how we eat, but they
also indicate how we feel about the rituals of food
preparation.

Kitchens in America have become a favorite topic of
discussion recently, and kitchen equipment has a secure
niche in technological achievement. In the introduction
to this book I explained how the American kitchen has
made almost a full circle in the last three hundred years.
We may not be sleeping in our kitchens again (although
my son does have a loft in his), but they have definitely
become gathering places once more. How we plan our
work space is a strong statement on our commitment to
eating well.

In this chapter I'd like to give you some ideas on how
you can create a more workable kitchen by incorporating
some of the efficiencies of modern technology and architectural design. By efficiency I don't mean living from
the freezer to the microwave, nor accumulating a room-
ful of tricky kitchen gadgets that require more energy.
Rather, I am concerned with the work flow of the modern
kitchen, with creating space relationships for each movement, with saving time and motion that can then be used
for more and better food preparation or other activities.
The workable kitchen should be a studio, not a clinic, for
food preparation.

Contemporary kitchen design is based on two very simple concepts. The first is the inner relationship of the
work centers, especially the sink, refrigeration, and cooking areas, with the objective being that food preparation
should be as rhythmic and effortless as possible. The sec-

ond concept is that space and storage should be planned so that things are kept near the point where they first come into use or where they are needed.

The major considerations anyone confronts when designing a new kitchen, or remodeling an old one, are covered in the following pages. There is a general discussion of kitchen needs followed by three examples of modern workable kitchens. The first, the Pullman Kitchen, a remodeled small kitchen that relies on most of the existing cabinetry and appliances, is best suited to a small family, working person, or couple. The second, the Family Kitchen, is built to specification and with an eye to extensive food preparation. The third, the Efficiency Kitchen, is a common design in modern houses, but has some added conveniences well suited for older and retired persons. I use these three plans, all of which are real kitchens, because they are suited to very different family sizes and lifestyles, but there are all kinds of options for the arrangement of a kitchen. You may have an old kitchen (as I have) and are interested in only a few minor changes to improve the work flow. However, if you combine them with a few decorative additions (see Chapter Six), you may find you have an entirely new outlook on food preparation. I think that nowhere in the house are small improvements felt as much as in the kitchen.

The following pages also offer some general consumer information on kitchen design. I hope they help you amend the workability of your studio.

WORK CENTERS

The three principal work centers are the sink, range, and refrigerator; they should be situated to create an easy work flow, and there should be proper storage around each area.

The sink center accommodates food washing and trimming (and, if desired, a dishwasher and garbage disposal). Counters are needed on either side of the sink, one for stacking dirty dishes, the other for draining washed dishes or as a place to set the dishes that have been removed from the dishwasher. Usually the dishwasher is placed on the left-hand side of the sink, although sometimes existing kitchen design or left-handedness may reverse the position, as in the Pullman Kitchen and the Efficiency Kitchen. A garbage disposal is not an essential, although it is often desirable in apartment kitchens. However, I have never had a garbage disposal and have little interest in one. If you are composting for a garden, you will have little need for a disposal unit. Pull-out bins on tracks under the sink are very convenient, and one can be located under the food-cutting area for wet garbage, as in the Pullman Kitchen and the Family Kitchen.

The refrigeration center should be near enough to the food preparation area (especially a cutting area) to save steps. It helps, too, to have some counter area next to the refrigerator for unloading groceries. As almost everyone knows, the refrigerator and stove should not be set side by side because the cooling function of the refrigerator works on dissipating heat, and the conflict between the two is hard on the mechanics of the refrigerator, so that consequently the refrigerator draws more power. For the same reason, the refrigerator should not be next to the water heater or dishwasher.

The cooking center should have easy access to the food preparation center, and, if possible, there should be counter area on either side of the cooktop. One of these counters should be heatproof to handle dishes coming directly off the stove or from the oven.

Optional work centers in the kitchen are a baking area, an eating area, an office area, and a gathering area. The baking area can be the food preparation area by the sink as mine is (under which I store baking appliances and tools), or it can be a separate area. In a special baking area with more counter space, you may want to keep the baking equipment on top of the counter—perhaps recessed for cleanliness.

A large kitchen offers many options for eating arrangements, but if you are working with small spaces, remember that each diner needs at least twenty inches of surface space for eating. In a small kitchen the problem is usually one of conflict with opening doors.

Space for an office is a wonderful addition to the kitchen, especially for the enthusiastic cook. The office space can be the place for your kitchen library, a blackboard, a bulletin board, a message center for the home. It's also a great place for kids to do homework.

If your kitchen opens onto the traditional family-room design of the 50s, you have a built-in gathering place. But if you are planning a kitchen that you want to be inviting, without its being too multipurpose, plan for sitting only — possibly a comfortable couch and dining chairs — and put the television and bookshelves elsewhere.

WORK SURFACES

Work surfaces in the kitchen should be durable since they take such a beating from water. Most of us have had experiences with painted-wood surfaces and know how difficult it is to keep inadequate counter materials clean and undamaged. The most common work surfaces are plastic laminate and ceramic tile, and some butcher-block areas. There are also those who opt for brushed steel or marble in the kitchen.

The advantages of ceramic tile are that the choices are many and the effect is warm and attractive. Tile is a lasting surface, and stain and heat resistant, but you must be careful not to slam down dishes or glasses. Laminated plastic also comes in many colors and patterns and with effects simulated to look like brick or wood. You can't be wildly careless with these surfaces either, as they can buckle and scar under extreme heat and hardy chopping. Butcher block looks wonderful and is very convenient for chopping and rolling out baked goods, but it burns and scars with use and tends to need frequent upkeep. Brushed steel does not scar like the old metal counters, and it's very good for receiving heat; however, I think an entire kitchen of metal is cold. Marble is beautiful, but also rather cold and quite expensive. It's best used in small areas, as in the Family Kitchen, because it can scratch with use and even crack if you are careless.

FLOORING

Floor surfaces are no less important than counters in the workable kitchen, and the options are much greater than they were twenty years ago. Imagine what your great-grandmother would have thought if she had walked into a carpeted kitchen.

Synthetic, stain-resistant floor coverings come in several substances, from the old-fashioned sheet linoleum to vinyl sheets and tiles to cork and asphalt tiles. Most people prefer sheet flooring with a hard finish that does not require waxing for spot resistance. The various synthetic tiles available are easier for the do-it-yourselfer to install, but they are not as durable as sheet flooring because they have a tendency to lift and collect moisture underneath. That is not true with ceramic tile, which comes in many sizes, designs, and finishes. While expensive, ceramic tile is resistant to any abuse. Wooden floors are once again popular in kitchens, and a polyurethane sealer will make a wood floor as resistant to stains and water as any synthetic flooring. Strong stain-resistant carpeting is available in various patterns and colors for kitchens, porches, and decks. The advantage of carpeting is that it is more noise resistant than most flooring and works well in smaller kitchens.

CABINETS

Kitchen cabinets, like work surfaces and flooring, come in various materials and styles. If you are starting over, the question is whether to buy prefabricated cabinets or have them made to your specifications. The decision is primarily financial since custom-built cabinetry is far more expensive. If your remodeling is only a limited operation, you can doctor up your existing cabinets with one of the new high-gloss paints and new hinges and knobs. And if you add a few new open shelves and some portable storage here and there, it's almost as if you had an entirely new kitchen (see the Pullman Kitchen).

Prefabricated cabinets are available in metal, wood, high-pressure plastics, and combinations thereof. They come in various sizes in width and depth, but the standard up-from-the-floor height is thirty-six inches with a countertop. However, if you have only the tiniest bit of carpentry skill you can raise or lower prefabricated cabinets to your desired height by mounting the cabinets on platforms or by cutting off some of the kick space below. Standard wall cabinets are designed to allow some space between the top of the cabinet and the ceiling — for storage (decorative or otherwise) or lighting. In order to achieve a continuous flow of cabinetry below, use filler strips, which are readily available.

Custom cabinets are desired not only for the workmanship and quality of material, but they fit the kitchen like a glove. If you have *any* carpentry talent and want to try your hand at some cabinetry for your kitchen, read the good instructional book listed at the end of this chapter.

In a small kitchen the "nonessential control" theory should be at work; that is, only the most-often-used appliances are needed. But when you are designing a kind of family dream kitchen, such as the Family Kitchen in this chapter, there is room to store less-often-used appliances and tools so they don't usurp work space or collect grease. Still, there are many modern kitchens that have more gadgets than the occupants ever use, so a frequent reevaluation of kitchen equipment is a good practice. The following paragraphs are concerned with the bigger, most common kitchen appliances — a range, refrigerator, dishwasher, and garbage disposal. When you are buying new appliances, remember that the choices are many and the price range is wide. It's wise to consult the ratings in a consumer publication for guidance (see Suggested Reading at the end of this chapter).

A cooking center is a must in a kitchen, but for some cooks the conventional stove has been replaced by a built-in cooktop and a microwave and/or convection oven. If you are remodeling a kitchen, my advice is not to buy a new range unless you need *more,* or *less,* cooking space. A good range, gas or electric, will last indefinitely if you are reasonably careful with it. The advantages of new ranges are primarily the self-cleaning ovens, removable parts for easy cleaning, and intricate timers. Recently the more expensive commercial-size ranges have become popular for home use; they offer warming ovens, some with downward ventilation. Also on the market now are gas ranges with spark igniters, which are energy efficient.

Kitchen refrigeration should be calculated on the size of the group using the kitchen. If you are buying a new

92

refrigerator, consider eight cubic feet of space for two people and add one cubic foot per person. This, however, is only a rule of thumb. It's ultimately one's lifestyle and interest in food preparation that determine the need for refrigeration or freezer space. Those who have kitchen gardens may want a larger freezer compartment for excess produce. And some people prefer a separate freezer since the temperature remains constant from less opening. In that case, a small refrigerator might be adequate. An automatic defrost refrigerator is a nice boon for busy people, and is commonplace now, but it *is* an energy consumer, as are ice makers.

A dishwasher is not an essential appliance, but it is a definite timesaver for a busy kitchen and is almost always included in the design of new homes. Also, many people invest in portable dishwashers for homes that do not have installation space. If you are adding a dishwasher to an old kitchen, it's customary to remove the bottom cabinet to the left of the sink, although there is no hard rule. New dishwasher models cut even greater corners by including food disposers that eliminate preliminary rinsing, and they have different cycles for fragile and heavy-duty washing. My mother uses her dishwasher just once a day — sometimes less — and she always stops the cycle to air-dry the dishes, thus saving heat energy.

Garbage disposals do not figure into a kitchen with a garden compost bin but are handy in apartment kitchens where it is difficult to dispose of wet garbage. In the past, one had to be careful with pits and stringy foods (not to mention silverware and goldfish), but the newer models will grind almost all food waste, and many operate on a continuous feed.

I must stress again that energy usage is an important consideration in planning a kitchen. It does not appear that costs will diminish — certainly not commensurate with the diminishing natural resources. Use only the power appliances you need the most to prepare a healthful menu, then you can, with the planet's blessing, feel virtuous every time you hand crank your food chopper or pasta maker, or cut and mix by hand. Why not think of food preparation as a dance, where all of your steps count.

The best lighting arrangement in the kitchen illuminates the entire room, with extra fixtures for special work areas. Unless your kitchen has particularly good natural light (for example, northern exposure or skylights), you will need some artificial lighting during the day too. Lighting needs are determined by room size, wall color, ceiling light, and eyesight. Many people prefer incandescent or track/spot lighting on work areas, especially if the fixtures can be located under a shelf to eliminate the direct harshness of the tubes. Installing lighting under shelves also eliminates shadows (see the Pullman and the Family Kitchens). Fluorescent lighting is cheaper than incandescent, but it's not as soft; and many people feel as I do, that it is hard on their eyes. If you are making lighting changes and are uncertain about how much lighting to add, consult an electrician or a store that specializes in lighting fixtures. They can help you determine how much wattage you need per square foot of your kitchen or work space.

VENTILATION

Most cooks agree that an adequate ventilation system is a necessary part of kitchen design. I agree, but I think it greatly depends on the indoor/outdoor air flow. A small apartment kitchen with one or no windows certainly benefits from direct ventilation over the stove or cooktop. As I mentioned earlier, some of the newer arrangements have fan systems directly in or beside the cooktop unit that draw grease and heat downward, but generally the ventilating system is located in the hood above the cooktop or in the wall. Occasionally ceiling fan systems are installed, but they must be quite powerful to draw up heat and odors. The two types of ventilation fans available are the ducted and nonducted, with variations on size, style, and price. The principle of the ducted fan is to draw heat and odors to the outside, using the shortest route possible, which is sometimes expensive. The ductless fan uses a filter and is less desirable because it can remove heat and moisture.

94

The three kitchens in this chapter have been designed with an eye to modern storage. Most of the storage in the Family and Efficiency Kitchens is built to specification, but the Pullman Kitchen, a remodeled kitchen, was created very economically and relies on many portable storage arrangements.

There are many creative products on the market that facilitate storage. Cookware and hardware stores, as well as kitchen catalogs, can give you a good idea of what is available. Following is a list of storage products that my friends and I have found useful:

Helper shelves, made of vinyl-coated steel rods, come in corner racks that enable you to stack three sets of dishes in one spot.

Expandable racks with legs that straddle items on a shelf below are space efficient.

Vinyl-coated steel shelving can be hung on doors and walls; some has locking baskets for adjustable spacing.

Aluminum shelving for the inside of pantry doors works well for storing small items or canned goods.

Metal hanging shelves for refrigerator storage hold loose items, bottles, and cans. They attach easily to existing refrigerator racks.

A pegboard is a great place for hanging pots, pans, and utensils; also small shelves can be hooked to it to hold spices and books.

Wide-spaced wall grid systems are available for hanging almost anything.

Creative wooden shelving for corner work areas can be made of expensive walnut or inexpensive stained pine.

Spice jars and small cans can be laid in drawers beneath work areas for easy accessibility. Dividers can be made of wood scraps.

Open-front plastic bins make good root-cellar storage on lower shelves away from the stove.

Bins can also be stacked against the wall; some made of plastic- or vinyl-coated metal are available with casters on the bottom bin.

Flatware holders mounted inside cupboard drawers or behind sink or work areas store small utensils.

A carousel for storing cooking tools and knives can be situated on a work counter or inside a tall shelf.

A solid plastic recipe file can be mounted beneath cupboards for hand use.

Organization of space beneath the kitchen sink is greatly aided by containers that attach to the cupboard doors. They are built of metal to accommodate trash bags or of solid plastic to hold plastic bags for wet garbage.

Another type of door-mounted unit can be used to hold dish-cleaning supplies.

Pull-out plastic trays are handy under the sink to hold cleaning compounds as well as to hold trash containers. One type of trash-bag container has one side cut out so it can be placed against the plumbing.

Vinyl-covered metal caddies are available for storing cleaning compounds and can be carried to where they are needed.

ENERGY-SAVING TIPS FOR THE KITCHEN

It may seem that creating a more workable kitchen is somewhat contradictory to conserving energy. Indeed, if one does not plan carefully that could be true. On the other hand, even if you add more electrical equipment to your kitchen, your energy bills will be lower if all the additions are fuel efficient and well planned. The owners of the Family Kitchen, which is a remarkably modern kitchen with a large refrigerator, cooktop, and two ovens, maintain that their energy bills are cut by half because of the efficiency of the arrangement, especially the coal-burning stove and the microwave conversion in the conventional oven. It's important to study the competition in fuel efficiency when you are buying new appliances. Meanwhile, here are a few suggestions for your existing kitchen that will lessen your energy bills.

1. As I mentioned earlier, the refrigerator should not be located next to the stove, dishwasher, or water heater. In fact, they should be as far apart as workability permits.

2. Keep your water heater at 120° (a little higher if you have a dishwasher), and wrap it in an insulation blanket, which is easy to install and will pay for itself rapidly.

3. When leaving home for any length of time, turn off your stove and water-heater pilot. Incidentally, my mother taught me very early to turn off the water hoses to the washing machine when they are not in use, especially if we were going to be out of the house since a break can cause a real disaster.

4. Use the kitchen ventilation fan only when absolutely necessary.

5. Keep your refrigerator running at a minimum — 0° F. in the freezer and 40° F. in the cold compartment. Keep coils clean and the door closures in good repair. Open the doors only when necessary. Because cold water will lower the interior temperature 10°, keep a gallon jar full of water in the refrigerator.

6. Run the dishwasher only when it is full, and try not to use the dry cycle. Instead, air-dry your dishes.

THE PULLMAN KITCHEN

This is a moderately remodeled apartment kitchen whose pullman style is common to many small houses and apartments. There can be doors at either end or, as in this case, one door from the dining area. The placement of the major work areas remains the same, but the remodeled work surfaces improve the flow of movement for food preparation. The original, small, twenty-inch stove and twenty-eight-inch separate freezer-refrigerator have been retained, but the old porcelain sink has been replaced with a double stainless-steel sink. A dishwasher has been installed to the right of the sink, but this is truly optional because the dishes could be drained on the new Formica counter.

The old linoleum flooring has been torn up to expose hardwood floors, which have been sanded, stained walnut, then covered with a polyurethane sealer for protection. Track lighting has been installed overhead, and incandescent lighting has been added under the sink-side shelves for spot lighting. All the existing cabinetry has been retained, but it has been painted a cream color with high-gloss, oil-base paint; new copper-finished metal pulls have been affixed to all the cabinetry. Kitchen walls and ceiling have been painted in a corresponding color in semi-gloss, oil-base paint.

On the sink side an eight-inch-deep bookshelf has been built against the end wall. It extends out over the board counter and runs from the top of the cabinets down to six inches from the counter. The original linoleum counter has been replaced with a cutting board to the left of the sink, but is separated from the stainless steel by two inches of Formica. The Formica covering has been laid around the sink and covers the entire length of the counter on the right side. The Formica also extends up six inches as a back splash along the length of the sink wall. These new work surfaces are trimmed with two-inch wood molding that runs the length of the sink-side counter. A painted wall extends up from the Formica to the cabinets, but it is separated by the same molding, which is attached horizontally to act as a spice shelf behind the cutting board and for miscellaneous storage on the other end.

Recessed wood half-shelves have been built into the upper cabinets on the right side of the sink for stacking bowls and cups, and a plastic holder for flatware has been mounted on the inside of one of the dish cupboard doors to free drawer space for pantry storage. Open storage/decorative shelves have been built above the sink, connecting the two cabinets.

Because the cutting board doubles as a baking counter, the cupboard below the left side of the cutting board is used for storing baking equipment. A plastic carousel full of food preparation tools sits on the cutting board to free the drawers on the lower right of the cutting board. The drawers have been turned into horizontal storage for canned goods and wine.

Rather than add a garbage disposal, the inside left cupboard door under the sink holds a portable garbage can, attached for easy accessibility to the cutting board and the sink. A portable plastic shelf unit has been attached to the inside of the right door to hold dishwashing items. A plastic pull-out tray with trash container has been installed under the right side of the sink, and under the left side, for storing cleaning compounds, there is a portable wire container, which can be carried around the house as it is needed.

On the lower right side of the sink, under the Formica

The Pullman Kitchen

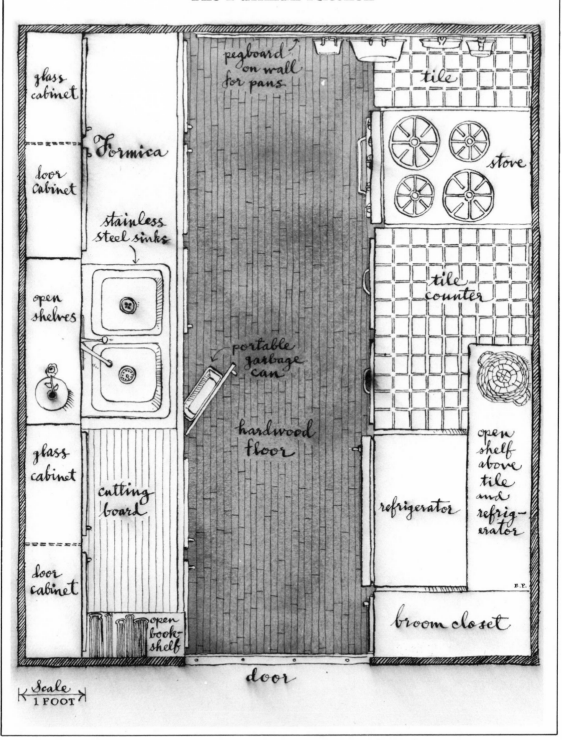

glass cabinet

door cabinet

open shelves

glass cabinet

door cabinet

Formica

stainless steel sinks

cutting board

open book-shelf

pegboard on wall for pans

portable garbage can

hardwood floor

tile

stove

tile counter

open shelf above tile and refrigerator

refrigerator

broom closet

B.P.

door

Scale
1 FOOT

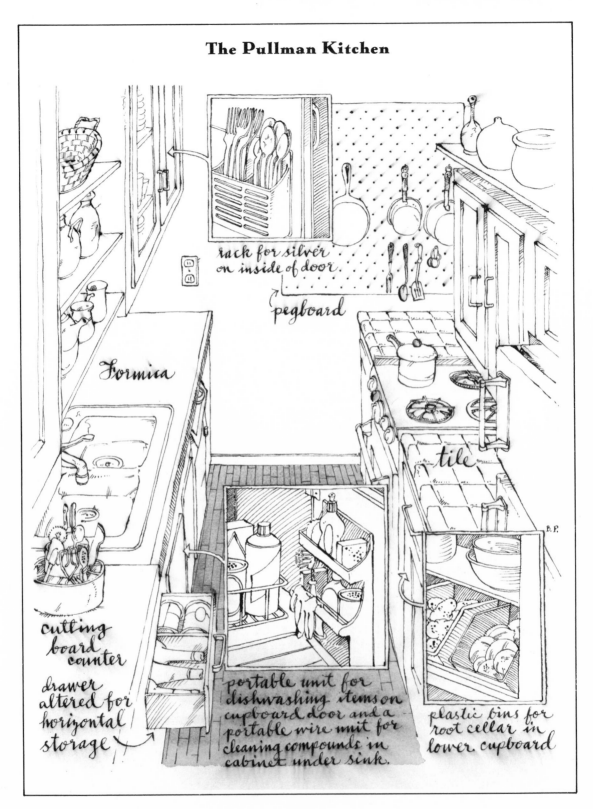

rack for silver on inside of door

pegboard

Formica

tile

cutting board counter

drawer altered for horizontal storage

portable unit for dishwashing items on cupboard door and a portable wire unit for cleaning compounds in cabinet under sink.

plastic bins for root cellar in lower cupboard

B. P.

counter, the cupboard has been replaced by a dishwasher, and the four drawers are used for horizontal can storage and for storing less-often-used kitchen items.

On the cooking side the linoleum counters on both sides of the stove have been tiled for accommodating hot pans. The tile has been extended up from the top of the stove and the work space to within eighteen inches of the ceiling. A wood shelf has been added at the top of the tile, running from the cabinets beside the refrigerator to the broom closet. The shelf provides a surface to which to affix a filter vent for the stove (a new addition) and for decorative storage. The tile is not necessary, but it provides a safe backdrop for the cooktop, or for a microwave or convection oven on the tile counter if one wished to place one there. The cabinet shelves to the left above the refrigerator remain the same as before but have been fitted with expandable helper shelves. The horizontal cupboard shelves under the small tile counter have been replaced with vertical partitions for storing flat pans and cookie sheets. Plastic bins have been fitted into the lower cupboard shelves next to the refrigerator for a root-cellar arrangement for vegetables. Pegboard has been attached to the wall at the end of the kitchen, extending over the tile counter. It has been painted the same color as the walls and is used for hanging all pots and pans.

THE FAMILY KITCHEN

This is a dream kitchen for the serious cook. It was designed by the owner with the help of an architect, and with occasional changes during construction, emerged a definite success. The family is extended in that the older children come home frequently. The owners entertain a great deal, both in the kitchen area and in the formal dining room. However, nuclear family life always centers around the kitchen for this family, and they tried to plan a kitchen with adequate gathering room.

Inclined to light and brightness, the owners opted for white walls and white-suede Formica counter tops. The cabinetry, made of paint-grade wood, is very professionally smoothed with three coats of white laquer. Track and spot lighting are used in the kitchen area, and skylights were installed in the eating area/family room. The floors are dark-stained hardwood with a polyurethane and wax finish. The entire area is heated by a fuel-efficient French stove that burns coal or wood. The use of butcher block in this kitchen is for warmth and not for chopping because the owner feels butcher block deteriorates too quickly under the knife. The fixed pieces of butcher block have been oiled with paraffin oil to preserve their quality, and a portable piece of butcher block is used for chopping. The owner moves it around the kitchen and will discard it when it becomes too marred.

Near the entry to the dining room is a 23.5-cubic-foot refrigerator with vertical freezer/refrigeration doors and ice-water and ice-cube dispensers built into the door. Beside the refrigerator is the baking section with a two-by-three-foot section of butcher block under which there is a pull-out bread board and four drawers of graduated sizes for baking tools. (The owner requested bread boards wherever possible for extra counter space.) Beside the butcher block is a recessed marble counter for rolling out dough. Under the marble counter are two tin-lined bins for flour with a deep, twelve-inch drawer underneath for larger baking items. A lazy-Susan cabinet utilizes the turn in the corner, adding more baking storage. Above the marble counter is a pass-through window that backs an armoire that acts as a serving cabinet for the formal dining room. The pass-through opening is covered with window shutters. Also, built up the side of the refrigerator are narrow shelves for tall bottles. Above the refrigerator is a storage cabinet, and running from that, around the corner to the oven, is a shelf used for decorative storage. There are large pieces of Mexican pottery, copper pans, and bowls.

Butcher block continues the counter to the oven. Above is a window opening onto a dining deck, and under the counter is a cabinet for vertical storage of cookie sheets and shallow pans, next to four drawers under a bread board. This kitchen has two ovens; the upper converts from conventional to microwave, and the lower oven is a smaller conventional oven. Above the ovens is a cabinet for grains and cereals; below is a drawer for pots and pans.

The Family Kitchen

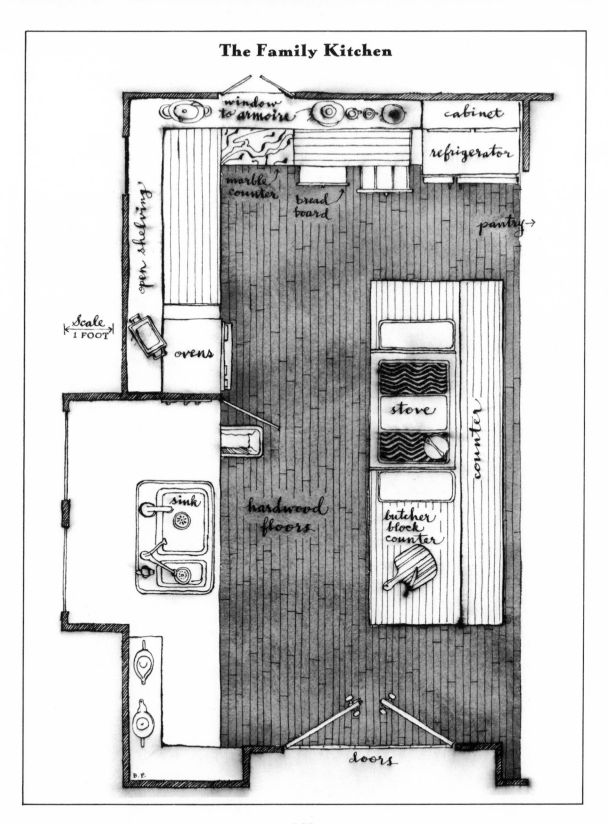

window to armoire

cabinet

refrigerator

marble counter

bread board

pantry→

open shelving

Scale
1 FOOT

ovens

stove

counter

Scale
1 FOOT

hardwood floors

butcher block counter

sink

doors

B.P.

The Family Kitchen

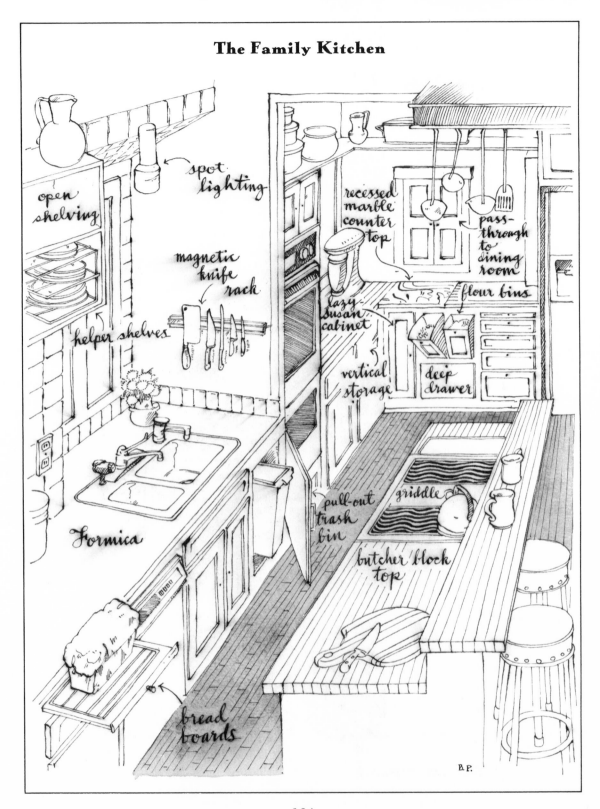

spot lighting

open shelving

magnetic knife rack

helper shelves

Formica

recessed marble counter top

pass-through to dining room

flour bins

lazy-susan cabinet

vertical storage

deep drawer

pull-out trash bin

griddle

butcher block top

bread boards

B.P.

There is a double stainless-steel sink — one side is eight by sixteen inches, the other is sixteen by twenty-one inches. The larger sink accommodates large pans. However, the owner now feels that a single large sink would have been adequate for everything because even more space would have been allowed. Vegetable washing could be done in a plastic colander that is stored under the sink. The larger sink has a garbage disposal. To the right of the sink is Formica counter under which is a pull-out trash bin. (The compactor is in the garage.) The owners did not install an opening in the counter, believing that odors would escape through it. Above, on the wall, is a magnetic knife rack. The cabinet under the sink is for storing dish-cleaning supplies, but it also houses a holding tank filled with water that is heated by a coil. The tank is connected to a faucet above to provide instant boiling water (the owners are avid tea drinkers). There is also a pull-out dishtowel rack under the sink.

To the left of the sink is a dishwasher with all the latest features, including a heat saver. Above is a window onto the dining deck; it is recessed to eighteen inches and decorated with Mexican tile. Tile is also used for the four-inch splash around the Formica counter space and extends up to the cupboards. Spot lighting above the sink is under a decorator shelf, which continues around the rest of the counter area.

Open shelving extends from the window around the corner to the door wall, except at the end where a six-foot mirror hangs. Under the counter is another bread board and additional drawers next to a cabinet that contains electrical gadgets. Between the kitchen counter and the heating stove French doors open onto decking.

The cooking area is an island with a four-burner restaurant-size cooktop, which has Z grates that disperse heat more effectively. (Pans can sit anywhere and absorb heat from the burners.) A griddle separates the burners, and a stainless-steel border extends around the cooktop. On both sides is more butcher block. The fan for the vent is on the roof to eliminate noise. Below the cooking area on the left are various side drawers for cooking tools and lids. Cabinets are below the actual cooking area, and there is a deep pan drawer on the top right and a bottom warming drawer. Utilizing a little extra space at this end of the island, the owner asked for a pull-out narrow drawer for trays, place mats, and so on. There is another similar arrangement behind this area that pulls out toward the outside door. There is an eating bar with stools behind the cooking island; the bar is raised four inches above the cooking area. It, too, is butcher block.

Next to the heating stove, which is recessed in tile, is a couch, coffee table, and lamp. A round table and six chairs are in the middle of the family room. On one wall is a French baker's shelf, which is used for decorative storage and plants since it gets good light from the skylights. Behind the shelf and to one side of the entrance from the dining room (actually under the stairs) is the pantry, which is lined with shelves; one section is enclosed and above an opening to the basement and functions as a cooler. The owners share a small office off the kitchen.

THE EFFICIENCY KITCHEN

This eight-foot-by-eleven-foot kitchen was designed with retirement-age occupants in mind. Although it is a developer's plan and no custom work is included, it's an efficient arrangement. With a little additional work by the new owners it has become perfectly adapted to their own personal needs.

A forty-two-inch-wide molded plastic counter runs the length of one side of the kitchen space. It divides the work area from the family room. The generous width allows for eating on the family-room side without interfering with the work space on the kitchen side. Also, the kitchen side of the counter has a slight rise at the edge to keep food and utensils from rolling off onto the floor.

The cabinets under the counter are the standard two-foot depth. They are backed with a retaining wall on the family-room side, allowing a ten-inch overhang for knee room underneath. The first change made by the new occupants was to the end cabinets. The doors were removed, and the four shelves were converted into drawers, using the cabinet fronts as drawer fronts, a much more convenient arrangement for the owners who found it difficult to rummage in the back of the lower cabinet. Two twenty-two-inch-wide drawers are above the converted

The Efficiency Kitchen

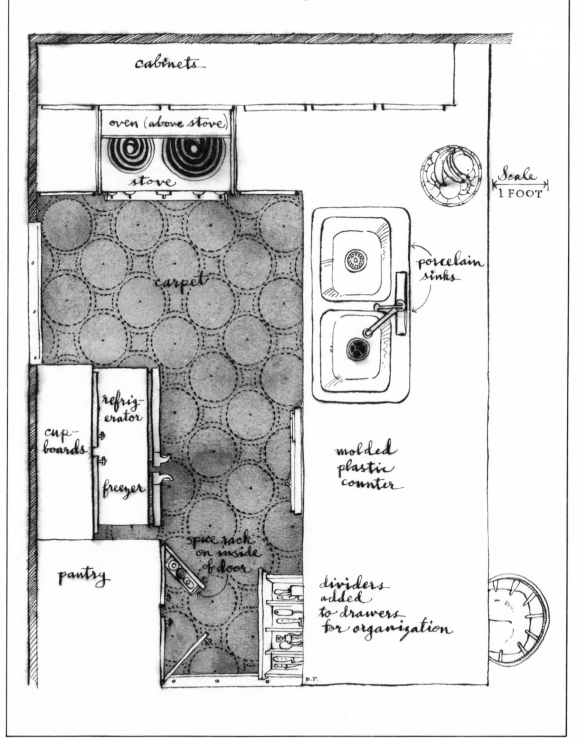

cabinets

oven (above stove)

stove

Scale
1 FOOT

porcelain
sinks

carpet

refrig-
erator

cup-
boards

freezer

molded
plastic
counter

spice rack
on inside
of door

pantry

dividers
added
to drawers
for organization

B.P.

The Efficiency Kitchen

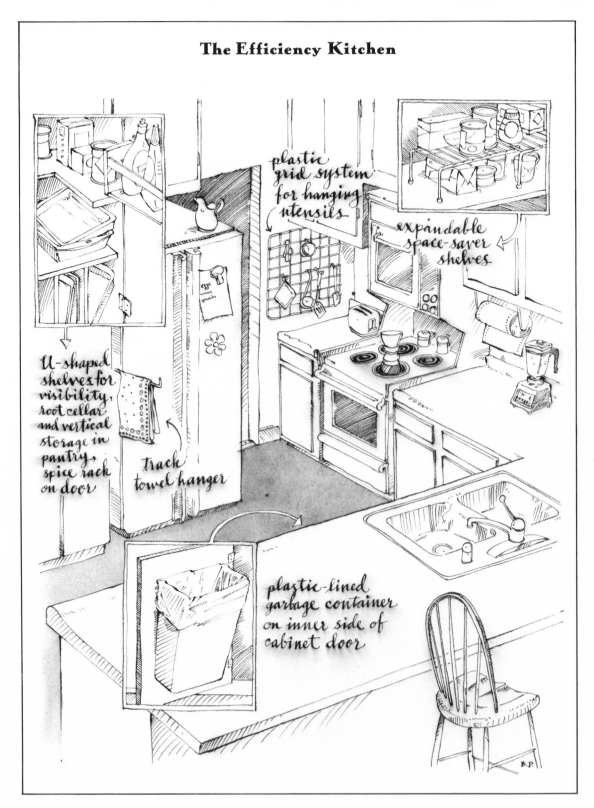

plastic grid system for hanging utensils

expandable space-saver shelves

U-shaped shelves for visibility, root cellar and vertical storage in pantry, spice rack on door

track towel hanger

plastic-lined garbage container on inner side of cabinet door

B.P.

cabinets and have been fitted with dividers for better organization. The dishwasher is to the right of the porcelain sink, which is a double with a garbage disposal. Because the owners have a large vegetable garden, most of their wet garbage is collected in a plastic-lined container attached to the inner side of a lower cabinet door and transferred daily to their compost.

The counter is L-shaped, circling around the sink and continuing to the cooktop surface. Upper cabinets on this side run thirty-six inches down from the ceiling and allow for equipment (blender, toaster oven, food processor) storage underneath, still allowing counter surface for work space. Four panels of neon lighting are centered in the kitchen ceiling, and one spotlight is directed to the counter space to the left of the sink. This lighting is adequate and saved the owners from having to add incandescent lighting under the upper cabinets, which would have been necessary without that light. The upper cabinets have three shelves and are twelve inches deep; they are dish cupboards and have been fitted with vinyl-coated portable racks for stacking cups and bowls. The lower cabinets under the counter are used for pots and pans and are rather awkward because they extend several inches into the corner under the turn of the counter. (Pipes to the sink occupy some of this space.) The owners may further improve the storage here by having a lazy-Susan shelf built to attach to the right-hand door of the cabinet. There are two drawers under the counter, both built with dividers for knives and utensils.

The cooking arrangement is a standard thirty-inch electric, four-burner cooktop with a lower oven. It is a drop-in arrangement but fits tightly within the cabinetry. There is a two-shelf oven that the owners use primarily because it's more convenient. To the left of the stove is more cabinetry. The upper three shelves are twelve by twelve inches, and the three drawers below are twelve by twenty-four inches. The counter top is the same throughout the kitchen, and the cabinets are all made of walnut-stained particle board. The owners have added pulls to all the cabinetry.

A door to the dining room divides the stove wall from the refrigerator. The refrigeration unit is twenty-one cubic feet, ample for garden freezing; and the freezer and refrigerator doors are side-by-side. There is a twelve-inch-by-thirty-six-inch cabinet above the refrigerator for less accessible storage. The refrigerator is separated from the pantry cabinet by a three-inch space. The owners have attached hanging storage hooks to the pantry cabinet and have installed a track towel hanger, which pulls out and is for dish-drying towels, which are used less often. (Hand towels are hung over a ring that is attached to the cabinets under the sink.)

The pantry cabinet (twenty-five by thirty inches) extends from the floor to the ceiling. The upper section is one large shelf (twenty-one inches high) and is used for storage of grains and flours. Vertical dividers have been built between the two bottom shelves to hold flat baking pans. The second shelf has been fitted with plastic bins for root-cellar storage of vegetables, and the two upper shelves have been replaced with U-shaped shelves for better visibility of stored items. These same upper shelves are recessed enough to allow built-in spice shelves on each cabinet door. All these changes were made by the same cabinetmaker and were not a major expense.

Indoor/outdoor carpeting in a spot-disguising pattern covers the kitchen floor area and is separated from the family room carpet by an aluminum kick. The owners find this a very handy kitchen for their age and lifestyle and like looking into the family room, with its fireplace, windows, and furniture, while they are working in the kitchen area.

Cabinet Making for Beginners. Drake Home Craftsman Series. Sterling Publishing Co.

Cook's Tools. Susan Campbell. Bantam Books.

Figi's Collection for Cooks (a catalog). Marshfield, Wisconsin.

Guide to Bathroom and Kitchen Remodeling. New Home Improvement Series. McGraw-Hill Publishing Co.

Planning and Remodeling Kitchens. Sunset Books. Lane Publishing Co.

Suggested Reading

Consumers' Buying Guide, Issue 1982. Consumer's Union Publisher.

Consumer's Digest 1982 to Discount Buying. Consumer's Digest, Inc.

Consumer Information

CHAPTER SIX
The Individual Kitchen
PERSONALIZING YOUR COOKING AND SERVING AREA

Chapter Six

The Individual Kitchen

"I love your kitchen," a friend remarked recently. "I love to sit here and look around while we talk." After a while she sighed, "Do you suppose that if I fixed up my kitchen, I could become a better cook . . . or like it better?" There was hope in that simple logic, and my answer was a quick, "Why not?" She is a bright woman, creative and active in many areas. Why couldn't she be just as successful in her kitchen?

We continued to talk while I worked. We had a glass of wine and discussed a wide variety of subjects — from the morality of women in politics to the versatility of the zucchini squash. By the end of her visit, I had prepared a meal for six people, and together we had managed to communicate a lot of ideas that were seemingly unrelated to the kitchen. But were they unrelated? After all, the original American kitchen functioned as a gathering spot for all family activity and conversation — the "common room," as I mentioned in the introduction. What better place, therefore, to discuss art and politics than in the warmth of the kitchen.

The kitchen was once, and can be again, the heartbeat of the home. It is, or should be, the place where nourishment begins, where food is prepared and served, and where friends and family join together in discussion and celebration. But now it can be even more than it was a hundred years ago. Not only do we have labor-saving tools and techniques to take the drudgery out of cooking, but the changing roles in the last ten years have brought so many men into the process of meal preparation. The kitchen can now be the "family room" in the truest sense.

115

In the previous chapters I have discussed nutrition, gardening, food purchasing and storage, food preservation, and kitchen design. The running theme in this book has been how to integrate these activities into the modern kitchen to make it a more efficient, healthful, and comfortable place to prepare food. While these subjects were all about making the most of technology, this chapter is concerned with balancing and off-setting the hard edge of that technology. By this I mean adding those personal touches that make your kitchen a warm and attractive place to work, gather, and celebrate. I think this part of creating "the whole kitchen" is the most fun.

DECORATING YOUR KITCHEN

What you can do to personalize your kitchen is not limited to square footage. Larger spaces may be a priority these days, but they are not always a possibility. A small kitchen can be very workable and attractive. I favor the "country-kitchen" look with an international flavor (that is, everything I like related to food and entertaining). However, I have seen all kinds of interesting ideas played up in kitchens — everything from ethnic to high-tech. I've been in kitchens that have built their images around personal collections — baskets, china, pottery, cookbooks, glassware, plants, even birds and fish. I visited a kitchen once that had one whole wall devoted to photographs of food which had been taken by the owner; another kitchen was filled with paintings and drawings of food, again made by the owners. But most of the visually interesting kitchens I've seen have been casual and varied.

My own kitchen is very small (eight by eleven feet), but I have still managed to cram in a lot of color and texture. By "cram" I mean that I have often been accused of having a neurosis over unused wall space, but I do love to be surrounded by lots of things. In fact, I can't add anything more to my kitchen walls and counters. I just have to rotate my treasures.

A cluttered kitchen is not pleasing to everyone, and is certainly not the prerequisite for the ultimately inviting kitchen. In fact, if you have all washable surfaces, the kitchen is the one room you can afford to make all white. The Family Kitchen in the preceding chapter has all-white surfaces and is very warm and inviting. There are small splashes of color, some plants, and windows that look out on greenery. It's a lively kitchen — full of people and good smells. It's the combination of good looks and good feeling that makes you want to gather in a kitchen.

I assume that most of us do not have unlimited capital to build a new kitchen or do one over in Mexican tile and copper, or marble and antiques, or new white Formica. Not many of us have a budget or room to build an open fireplace in the kitchen surrounded by old brick and knotty pine. Still, there are many ideas, quick and low cost, that will add charm to your kitchen and give it that well-used look. Your cupboards, for example — does that simulated wood veneer offend your love of the real stuff, or darken your small room? Take off the cabinet doors, or at least some of them, and display your kitchenware. Don't worry about spatters and grease collecting on the shelves — remember how much activity was going on in the old American kitchen. Of course, I'm not suggesting you hang your Picasso over the stove.

You can build some open shelves if you have some available wall space. I have a sizable collection of Mexican pottery and glassware, so I constructed a simple frame made of one-by-twelve-inch pine with two interior shelves. Then by mounting the frame twelve inches from the ceiling I ended up with four shelves for storage and display. The frame is attached to the wall with wood braces (1-3/4 by 1 inch) under the second and fourth shelves nailed into the studs and using molly bolts in-between. I use my dishes daily, so it is convenient as well as a colorful addition to my kitchen. Because of its location, it would have been cumbersome to have cupboard doors. I oiled the pine, but I have seen other open shelves that were painted to contrast with the contents. The Pullman Kitchen in Chapter Five has a similar shelf arrangement over the sink.

Open shelves can also be built to jar sizes if you have an odd collection. Save vitamin and condiment jars, and go around to restaurants and delicatessens to collect some of the larger jars from onions, cherries, pickles, pigs feet. They make good storage jars for grains and legumes, and you can paint the lids. Why should we hide good, basic foods in a closet. A painter doesn't hide his brushes and paints, nor a sculptor his materials and tools.

If appliances (stove and refrigerator) seem large and terribly white for your small kitchen, hang a bulletin board or a calendar or a poster on the door or side.

I like to hang kitchen items so they are handy. Wherever there is wood, I hang pots, pans, baskets, colanders, and small tools. My window frames are full of little items, and although my window frames are made of wood, this is also a good way to "warm up" aluminum windows in modern homes and apartments. (Remember, though, if you live in an apartment where there are rules about pounding nails or the walls are made of sheetrock and don't hold hooks or nails easily, Chapter Five has many suggestions for hanging things easily.)

Windowsills, too, make nice shelves for glass bottles to catch the light or fill with flowers or weeds. When I lived in Mexico years ago, I had a wonderful, large, recessed window over the sink with a tile shelf for ripening fruit and displaying pottery. A former resident had glued a sunburst design of broken glass on the window—those rich colors so peculiar to Mexico.

MAKING YOUR KITCHEN MULTIPURPOSE

Even though my kitchen is small and not wildly convenient by architectural standards, it still functions as a studio for me in that it has been the center of my life for the past ten years. In it I have tested recipes for seven cookbooks and countless newspaper and magazine columns, and it does have some very nice features. There is a large window overlooking the front deck and the beach houses across the street. Under the window is a long redwood counter for eating, and I use it for making notes too. In fact, I wrote the *Whole Earth Cook Book* there. I like to sit daydreaming at the window in the late afternoon, watching the people walk down to the beach at the end of the street.

Of course, a larger room has many advantages. Sometimes it's the only studio space in the house, and it's especially nice for those who like a little action while they are working, or feel they should be doing two things at once. I've known writers who have perfectly comfortable and quiet offices, but prefer to work at the kitchen table for the warmth and company. So if you have room for a drawing board, a sewing machine, a loom, or a piano, just think what you can get done in a day's time. Whether you are making pot holders or writing a symphony, you can be at it while the soup simmers, the bread rises, or the jam jells. (So who needs a microwave?) Or if you have been working away from home all day, you can relax with the newspaper or watch the news in the kitchen while something bubbles or broils.

I may be exaggerating a bit, but the point is that the kitchen does not have to be shut off from the general activity of a home. It can be the essence of the home, and by using your kitchen to its greatest potential, you can cut back on many so-called convenience appliances that are supposed to speed up food preparation. I'm not contradicting myself when I say there are many good labor-saving devices, and I'm not suggesting we return to stocking a wood stove, nor am I opting for a root cellar over refrigeration, nor for making everything from scratch. What I'm stressing is that if kitchen space is used to the fullest, we can save time and labor as efficiently as if we had every kitchen gadget on the market. And at the same time we can involve ourselves in other creative activities. The multipurpose kitchen allows us to make a small, but definite, commitment to the conservation of energy; it allows us more involvement in the full cycle of food preparation; and it can also allow us artistic expression quite unrelated to cooking.

CELEBRATING IN YOUR KITCHEN

In the introduction to this book I talked about the disappearance of the main meal as a gathering point in the family day. I am not alone when I say that this has been a great loss to American home life. Many people feel that as a nation built on the family unit we desperately need special moments together each day. It is not a need or custom peculiar only to this country; gathering for meals is an international habit. Interestingly enough, when the young Americans of the 60s moved onto rural communes or established communal living arrangements in urban areas, the main meal of the day was one of their most important rituals. A sit-down meal is a perfect time to bring a living group together for reorientation and communication. The meal does not necessarily have to be in the evening. It's the gathering together that is important. There is nothing more humanly unifying than a pause before a leisurely meal and another moment of pause afterwards.

The way in which you serve a meal matters as much as the content of the menu. Whether you eat in the kitchen or not, try to make the dining area as attractive as the rest of your food preparation area. If you prefer china or pottery, fine linen or coarse-woven fabric, your dining table should be a worthy completion to a well-prepared meal. Don't save the creative touches just for guests; make every meal a feast: candles, flowers, colorful place mats, tablecloth, and napkins. (Cloth napkins can be used several times before they are laundered if each person has a special color or napkin ring.) My mother tells a sweet story of how her father always insisted on a linen napkin for himself at every meal in their simple, frame farmhouse on the North Dakota prairie. He had an elaborate silver ring with a little china vase attached. She remembers gathering violets in the spring to put in the vase.

Serving a meal with style is the nicest complement to good food. If the kitchen is a place where the family and guests like to gather before the meal, the dining table should be a place where they all want to linger after they have eaten. As Walt Whitman so gently wrote:

After the supper and talk—after the day is done
As a friend from friend his final withdrawal prolonging.

Appendix

Everyone knows nowadays that we in the United States are in the process of making a major change that will affect all parts of our lives. It is the conversion from the U.S. Customary System of weights and measures to the decimal-based Metric System. The Metric System has always been a part of the language of the scientist, but it is now time to internationalize that tool. Not only is the Metric System more logical to teach and understand, but it makes perfect sense to have a common system of weighing and measuring when there is so much trade taking place between countries.

I am including a table of conversions for basic weights and measurements that are used in cooking. You will see in the table of U.S. Customary Measurements how much arithmetic must be done to change a teaspoon to a cup, for example; but how simple it is to change one metric value to a larger metric value — you simply move the decimal point one place to the right. Metric units are measured in tens, and the relationships are easy to see and understand.

Note that the conversion factor used in these tables is not exact. The metric value is rounded off to make it more convenient to work with and remember. A cup, for instance, is given here as 2.40 deciliters rather than as 2.365835 deciliters.

Someday we will have gram scales as part of our basic kitchen equipment. A liter will no longer be thought of as a little more than a quart, or a kilo as just over two pounds; they will simply be a liter and a kilo.

In the Metric System the *meter* is the fundamental unit of length, the *liter* is the fundamental unit of volume, and the *kilogram* is the fundamental unit of weight. The following prefixes, when combined with the basic unit names, provide the multiples and submultiples in the Metric System.

milli — one thousandth (.001)
centi — one hundredth (.01)
deci — one tenth (.1)
deca — ten (10)
kecto — one hundred (100)
kilo — one thousand (1,000)

Volume Conversions (Capacity)

Tea-spoons (tsp.)	Table-spoons (tbsp.)	Fluid Ounces (fl. oz.)	Cups (c.)	Pints (pt.)	Quarts (qt.)	Deci-liters (dl.)	Liters (l.)
1	1/3	1/6	1/48			.05	.005
3	1	1/2	1/16			.15	.015
6	2	1	1/8	1/16		.30	.030
12	4	2	1/4	1/8		.60	.060
24	8	4	1/2	1/4	1/8	1.20	.120
36	12	6	3/4	3/8	3/16	1.80	.180
48	16	8	1	1/2	1/4	2.40	.240
				1	1/2	4.80	.480
				2	1	9.60	.960

Note: Do not confuse the present British System with the Metric System. British countries use the same system of weights we do, but their cooking utensils (cups and spoons) are slightly larger than those used in the United States and Canada. British countries, also, are now converting to the Metric System.

Weight Conversions (Mass)

U.S. Customary Units		Metric Equivalents	
Ounces (oz.]	Pounds (lb.)	Grams (g.)	Kilograms (kg.)
1/2	1/32	14.175	.014
1	1/16	28.35	.028
4	1/4	113.40	.113
8	1/2	226.80	.227
12	3/4	340.20	.340
16	1	453.60	.454

1 kilogram (1,000 grams) equals 2.2 pounds.

Fahrenheit and Celsius (often known as Centigrade) temperatures may be converted by using the following simple equations.

$$Fahrenheit = 9/5\ Celsius + 32°$$
$$Celsius = 5/9\ Fahrenheit - 32°$$

°F.	°C.	°F.	°C.	°F.	°C.
-40	-40	149	65	329	165
-31	-35	150	65.5	338	170
-22	-30	158	70	347	175
-13	-25	167	75	350	176.6
-4	-20	176	80	356	180
0	-17.7	185	85	365	185
5	-15	194	90	374	190
14	-10	200	93.3	383	195
23	-5	203	95	392	200
*32	*0	212	100	400	204.4
41	5	221	105	401	205
50	10	230	110	410	210
59	15	239	115	419	215
68	20	248	120	428	220
72	22.2	250	121.1	437	225
77	25	257	125	446	230
86	30	266	130	450	231.1
95	35	275	135	455	235
100	37.7	284	140	464	240
104	40	293	145	473	245
113	45	300	148.9	482	250
122	50	302	150	491	255
131	55	311	155	500	260
140	60	320	160	600	315.5

As you may have noticed, oven gauges (Fahrenheit scale) begin at 150° (or warm) and increase by 25° to 550° or 600° (or broil). Celsius gauges will probably be numbered from 65° to 315°.

*Water freezes at these temperatures.

Index

About the Author

Sharon Cadwallader was born in North Dakota and raised in southern California. Her career in food writing began in 1970, when she helped found the Whole Earth Restaurant on the campus of the University of California at Santa Cruz; from this grew her first cookbook, *The Whole Earth Cookbook* (coauthored with Judi Ohr). Still in print, *The Whole Earth Cookbook* has sold more than a quarter of a million copies in several editions.

Sharon's subsequent books, nine in all, include *In Celebration of Small Things, Whole Earth Cookbook 2, Sharon Cadwallader's Complete Cookbook,* and *Cooking Adventures for Kids.* In recent years she has written a monthly column for *Bon Appetit* magazine and many feature articles on food and restaurants; her weekly column, "Naturally," is syndicated through the *San Francisco Chronicle* to over 100 newspapers throughout North America. Sharon is currently developing a children's cooking program for television. She lives with her son, Leland, in Santa Cruz, California.